WINNING
the SECOND
CIVIL WAR

WINNING

the SECOND

CIVIL WAR

WITHOUT FIRING *a* SHOT

JIM HANSON

EDITED BY: LTC SAMANTHA NEROVE, USA, RET.

REPUBLIC
BOOK PUBLISHERS

WINNING *the* SECOND CIVIL WAR

FIRST EDITION

Copyright 2021 Jim Hanson

Hardcover ISBN: 9781645720423

Ebook ISBN: 9781645720430

For inquiries about volume orders, please contact:

Republic Book Publishers

501 Slaters Lane #206

Alexandria VA 22314

editor@republicbookpublishers.com

Published in the United States by Republic Book Publishers

Distributed by Independent Publishers Group

www.ipgbook.com

Book designed by Mark Karis

Printed in the United States of America

CONTENTS

INTRODUCTION

AMERICA IS FIGHTING A SECOND CIVIL WAR for the heart of this country. This book is about how we on the Right can win it without firing a shot.

The long political battle between Conservatives and Liberals has turned into a much uglier and dangerous form of conflict, even open violence at times. There is little common ground remaining when every aspect of life has become polarized and politicized. That is not going to change any time soon. If we don't marshal our forces and learn how to operate effectively in this new type of warfare, we will lose to the activist Left.

It will take major changes to the political, professional, and cultural institutions we have relied on for half a century. They have failed us. We must build better organizations more suited to the battles we are currently fighting. We have the fundamental advantage that our principles, which come from America's founding and God, are far better than theirs drawn from Socialism. But, we must have the proper troops, weapons, strategy, and tactics to win. Working together we can build a path to victory.

I'm a team player. Politics and governance is a team sport and I've fought for and defended our team even when I was unhappy or disillusioned with it. It has always been far better than the alternative. Now it's time to face the fact that the current structure of the Right isn't up to the task at hand. Our enemy is very good at what they do so we need to up our game to beat them.

That's not to say the institutional Right as a whole has failed. It will always have one of the greatest victories in human history to its credit, defeating the Soviet Union in the Cold War without firing a shot. That was a conflict with the potential to end in nuclear Armageddon, killing everyone on the planet. The free countries of the West led by the political will, military might, and economic power of the American conservative movement did that. The world should be forever grateful.

There has also been a long-simmering, internal Cold War between Liberals and Conservatives since those days as well. The problem is only the Left has really been acting like it. They want to replace our Founding principles with Wokeness, the newest brand of Socialism. The Right says if it ain't broke, don't break it. But we have not moved to a wartime footing.

They have recruited, organized, and deployed their forces with a shared mission of fundamentally transforming America. They truly believe America is a fatally flawed nation that must be destroyed so a socialist paradise can be built on the ashes. They are wrong, but they were winning until just recently.

The past five years have seen our internal Cold War flare up into the first stages of a Second Civil War with Left and Right substituting for the North and South.

They are zealots and this is not just politics as usual to them. They are convinced we on the Right are evil and must be stopped. They have lost the ability to agree to disagree. If you are on the opposite side of an issue from them, they condemn you a racist, White Supremacist, misogynist homophobic hater, and the list goes on. They are not willing to coexist with you any more than they would tolerate Adolph Hitler. It is their secular religious mission to demonize, destroy, and eradicate us. They do not want to coexist with either the Judeo-Christian values that formed the basis of Western Civilization or the actual religious believers who make up much of the Right. The sooner we understand, acknowledge, and act accordingly, the better chance we have to survive.

The Second Civil War is the battle of freedom vs. state control. Let's pray it doesn't turn into a full-on shooting war, but a look at the past year shows we're well down that path.

The Left continues their totalitarian pursuit to marginalize and crush anyone who doesn't toe their party line. With history as a great predictor of the future, regimes based on Socialism never worked well. The oppressed rise up. Those of us on the Right will not quietly or passively submit to the boot of state control the Left is aiming to bring down on our necks.

Winning this second civil war while avoiding open conflict is the purpose of this book. We have avenues open to us to fight back without violence. They are not as glorious as shouting "Wolverines!" as the righteous resistance like the kids in the movie *Red Dawn*. The options we should pursue fall well short of armed insurrection, which avoids any legal complications.

We have the winning ideas. We will prevail with them but to do so we will have to fight much smarter tactically and strategically on both offense and defense.

We will examine three things as we plan our counteroffensive.

Part I delves into the history and development of America's internal battles after World War II. In the late 1940s, both Left and Right chose missions and built institutions to carry them out. The Left chose domestic policy and the Right took national security and business.

We were fighting a Cold War against the Soviet Union and simultaneously an internal Cold War at home. We'll see how the Left was very successful in their covert efforts to revamp our entire social structure and culture. We'll also examine the course of the institutional Right. Then look at the victories as well as the mistakes that have led us to our current failing position.

Part II will examine the shift from internal cold war to more active conflict which began with the election of President Barack Obama. He took the activist Left and stoked the fires of grievance. Then he launched them against the country demanding not just change, but a fundamental transformation of America. The answer to Obama and the decades of weakness and retreat by the Republican establishment was the rise of President Donald Trump and the fighting wing of the Right. We'll look at how this has unfolded and how close we really are to a true Second Civil War.

Part III is the counterattack. We will identify the types of political, cultural, civic, and professional institutions we need to win. There must be infrastructure and a platform that appeals to our changing demographics. We have ceded the war on the home front to the Left for far too long as we focused our energies on keeping the world safe for democracy. The American Dream is now in jeopardy.

We have lost a number of battles but the war for the future of America is not lost. They roused the big dogs from the porch and now they will deal with the consequences. It's time for the Right to fight. And win.

PROLOGUE

THE CHANTS OF "USA! USA! USA!" echoed on the walls of the Capitol that first week of 2021. Protestors were angry about an election they felt was stolen. They pushed through the barricades and the thin line of Capitol Police was quickly overwhelmed. The crowd began to pour up the steps and onto the balconies overlooking the National Mall toward the Washington Monument. They hung a giant American flag from the balustrade on the top balcony.

Others broke into the main building after smashing windows or forcing doors open. Within a short time, the entire police presence had retreated deep inside. The storming of the Capitol stopped the counting and certification of the Electoral College slates inside. This was not a stated goal of the event organizers or the speakers who preceded the march, but it happened nonetheless.

The infiltrators quickly spread throughout the building and the members of Congress were evacuated. Then the photo opportunities began. A picture on the dais usually occupied by Speaker Nancy Pelosi in the House chamber was especially prized, although it seems she took her big gavel with her when she left. The Speaker's office was one of the few places any real damage was done. She was one of the least favorite among the MAGA crowd and they showed it.

Sadly, the protest was not without casualties and there were a number of violent acts that deserve the full penalty of the law. A Capitol Police Officer died after struggling with protesters and others were attacked; and, Ashli Babbit, an Air Force veteran, was shot and killed while entering the building. She was not known to be armed and the investigation into her death is ongoing.

Several hours later reinforcements from the National Guard and other police agencies arrived and they began clearing the building. Soon after that it was over.

The Storming of the Capitol will become an iconic moment in our nation's history for good or ill. Many of the folks wearing red, white and blue that day would say it was citizens reminding their government they would not be ignored and their concerns about an election being stolen would be addressed. The media, Democrats, and some Republicans have called them a mob, an insurrection, and even domestic terrorists.

The reaction from the Left was hardly unexpected. They were horrified by mob violence for a political cause. But where was this outrage during the 2020 riots? Where was this condemnation when Black Lives Matter and Antifa rioted, looted, burned and even killed people for months throughout 2020? Why were they not called a mob, an insurrection, or domestic terrorists?

Those are entirely fair questions to ask. It is wrong to break and enter property even if people feel their cause is just. The rioters at the Capitol earned the names they were called, but so did BLM/Antifa during their rampages of destruction. And in both cases the violent ones were a small percentage of relatively peaceful crowds.

Some have said the act of entering the Capitol building made that a much more offensive act than burning and looting mere businesses. Sen. Dick Durbin (D, IL) said:

> This is a special place. This is a sacred place. But this sacred place was desecrated by a mob today, on our watch. This temple to democracy was defiled by thugs.

That is an absurd bit of sanctimony. So, Dick, are you saying you're the Cardinal of the Capitol? We don't worship government in this country. At least on the Right we don't. Yes, it is the nation's house, but spare us the self-serving hyperbole. Ask any business owner which is worse, the mob burning their business, livelihood, and means of supporting their families to the ground or a mob destroying Capitol property.

Why is occupying and not looting the Capitol somehow more heinous than destroying the livelihood of thousands of regular Americans? The entire life's work of far too many entrepreneurs went up in flames in 2020. They were forced to watch protestors, rioters, and mobs break their windows and steal, destroy, and burn everything they had while the local police were told to stand down.

Compare that to some members of Congress who were protected by their own police force, evacuated to safety immediately, and mildly inconvenienced before returning to work a few hours later none the worse for wear.

President-elect Joe Biden emerged from his basement lair where he had spent the campaign. He immediately began using divisive rhetoric and injecting race into an event that had zero racial aspects.

> No one can tell me that if it had been a group of Black Lives Matter protesters yesterday that they wouldn't have been treated very differently than the mob that stormed the Capitol.

Then he began demagoguing the people who protested at the Capitol.

Don't dare call them protesters, Mr. Biden said in remarks from Wilmington, Del. They were a riotous mob. Insurrectionists. Domestic terrorists. It's that basic. It's that simple.[1]

Racial grievance mongering and demonizing the forces of the Right are connected for him. Biden also announced he would be making a major priority of fighting domestic terrorism. But he and the Left are not interested in treating all acts of political violence equally. Neither Biden nor anyone else from the Left called the 2020 riots by Black Lives Matter and Antifa domestic terrorism even though 25 people died, 700 law enforcement officers were injured and more than 150 federal buildings were attacked.[2,3]

Democrats in Congress immediately jumped at the opportunity for a last chance to impeach President Trump. They had previously failed in their four-year-long quest to take out the Republican president. They never accepted the results of the 2016 election or his presence in the White House. The Democrats wasted millions of taxpayer dollars to impeach a sitting president but found no crimes he committed during their exhaustive multiyear pursuit. Their quest ended in acquittal. They saw Trump's role in the protest at the Capitol as their last shot at taking him down.

They filed Articles of Impeachment charging him with "willfully inciting violence against the government of the United States." Impeachment is a political act by its nature, but this was a stunningly partisan attack. Coming barely 10 days before Biden's inauguration made it clear and evident it was pure revenge, not any kind of justice. They wanted to remove Trump from office before his term ended to delegitimize his entire Presidency.

Trump didn't help himself by pushing some of the least supportable theories in his claims the election was stolen and that he had actually won in a landslide. Although unhelpful to the political climate, he had every right to contest the election. That included challenging the counting of the Electoral College ballots. Unless the Constitution was stealthily edited, the President enjoys the same free speech rights we all do.

While speaking to the protesters who were rallying at the Washington Monument prior to a planned march to the Capitol, President Trump said:

> I know that everyone here will soon be marching over to the Capitol building to peacefully and patriotically make your voices heard…
>
> And we're going to cheer on our brave senators and congressmen and women and we're probably not going to be cheering so much for some of them. Because you'll never take back our country with weakness. You have to show strength and you have to be strong.[4]

That is simply not incitement by the standard set by the Supreme Court in Brandenburg v. Ohio which requires a direct statement calling for violence. He literally says, "peacefully and patriotically make your voices heard." But that doesn't matter to the unhinged Democrats in Congress or to the tech tyrants of Silicon Valley who run our digital town squares.

Twitter, Facebook and Instagram began purging Conservatives immediately after the events at the Capitol. Twitter permanently banned the personal account of the President of the United States and many other high-profile people on the Right, including retired Lieutenant General Michael Flynn.

No due process, no hearing, or appeal. The tech giants own the free marketplace of ideas and acted with impunity. These are the actions of petty tyrants, dictators and totalitarian states. Welcome to the new world where a small collection of companies control who can speak to the public on the most widely used sites.

The social media companies hated that President Trump used their platforms as a way to speak directly to the people and avoid the media filter. But they needed him. When he began using Twitter as his main speech outlet during the 2016 presidential campaign, their business was floundering and investors were worried. Trump made Twitter the place to be and their growth and stock price have been on fire ever since.

President Trump was on his way out of office but they were determined to hurt him. They were so obsessed they were reading his tweets like tarot cards. The President tweeted the following completely inoffensive message:

> To all of those who have asked, I will not be going to the Inauguration on January 20th.[5]

As part of their rationale for permanently suspending him, Twitter posted this insane bit of mindreading:

> The second Tweet may also serve as encouragement to those potentially considering violent acts that the Inauguration would be a safe target, as he will not be attending.[6]

Together the tech tyrants banned millions of accounts with hundreds of millions of followers. They decided to exercise their monopoly power in a partisan purge to shut down voices and ideas they disagree with. As private companies they can do as they wish, but their terms of service say they will treat people equally. They opened themselves up to lawfare as people will undoubtedly exercise their rights under consumer laws to be treated with good faith.

The Left likes to remind us if we don't like how these companies operate, we are free to set up our own social media. That is true as long as they aren't violating antitrust law. But members of the Right did set up a competitor to Twitter called Parler, and it was doing very well.

Parler promised no viewpoint discrimination or censorship and that was welcome news. Conservatives flocked to it as they tried to avoid having their voices silenced. But after the incident at the Capitol, in the middle of the great purge of conservative accounts from social media, the tech tyrants struck.

Google banned the Parler app from its store, then Apple followed suit and finally Amazon pulled their web-hosting services. If that is not a conspiracy to stifle competition, I don't know what is. Parler is working to overcome that, but it has been severely limited in its ability to run its business.

The Left is using all the tools at their disposal to shut down and isolate all of us on the Right. During 2020, their allies BLM and Antifa terrorized the entire country causing billions of dollars in damages. The Left's media and social media allies influenced the election by censoring and spinning information damaging to their preferred candidate Biden and pushed information damaging to President Trump. They have gone even farther down the path toward their totalitarian utopia and are now using their powers to silence and even criminalize conservative thought.

This will not stand.

The danger of things spinning out of control is increasing every day. Our window to stop it is limited. If we are to avoid open conflict, we must turn the tide quickly.

In this book, we will examine and discuss the current dangers. What are the proper classifications for the violence being done by the Left and Right? What are the ground rules? Most importantly, what can we do to stop it from escalating into a full-scale Civil War?

Then we will launch a plan to win this war for the stability of our country and defeat them before the figurative battles turn literal.

PART I

THE AMERICAN COLD WAR

DEVELOPS (1950-2008)

BOTTOM LINE UP FRONT

Part I examines the root causes and historical timeline of the current conflict. It details the growing divergence in views about America between the political Right and Left. We were fighting an external Cold War against an external enemy, the Soviet Union. While we were rightly focused on that, the Left was fighting an internal Cold War to fundamentally transform American institutions.

The modern welfare state was the fork in the road that led to many of the cultural pathologies that infect the country today. The Left was successful in absorbing our education systems, popular culture, media, and government bureaucracy. The Right successfully defeated the Soviet Union. Losing them as an enemy took away the unity of purpose we on the Right found in fighting Communism.

After President Ronald Reagan, the two Bush presidencies floundered as Democrat-Lite domestically; and replaced Communism with terrorism as the boogeyman. We then meandered into nation-building and accomplished very little beyond decades-long wars in Iraq and Afghanistan we've been unable to win.

The Left continued its surreptitious slide toward socializing our country. Our culture was moving leftward at a steady pace resulting in powerful changes that weren't so glaring as to draw everyone's attention. The Left's stealth made it difficult to get people on the Right to acknowledge and react to the danger.

Andrew Breitbart, founder of Breitbart News and a cofounder of HuffPost, said, "Politics is downstream to culture." The Left has spent decades dominating the main organs of American culture and our political infrastructure began to reflect that. The country as a whole continued to move further and further to the Left.

That era ended and the American Cold War began to flare up when Barack Obama was elected President in 2008.

1

THE SIDES WE CHOSE

AN UNWRITTEN UNDERSTANDING developed post World War II where Democrats took the lead on domestic issues while Republicans handled national security and business. This didn't seem like a bad deal for the Right. We had just won the biggest war ever but the Soviet Union and Communist China were still existential threats. We took the important jobs: keeping the world and America safe for Democracy and building the infrastructure of the American Dream. The Left knew they had the better part of the deal and they had a covert plan. They began a fundamental transformation of this country from the inside.

THE ACADEMIC ENTERTAINMENT COMPLEX

As Conservatives and Liberals set about their chosen tasks, they built institutions and developed cadres to staff them. The Left started in Academia and began changing our universities to fit their agenda. Those went from places grounded in classical liberal thought paired with rigorous programs in science and the arts to laboratories for radical ideas that could only survive in that protected environment.

Academic tenure afforded activist academics insulated freedom. They used it to grow programs of study designed to take us to a brave new world. They were developing the intellectual framework for dismantling the bedrock principles of western society. They wanted state control of an unruly population that could not be trusted to do the right thing on its own. It was a path to Socialism, the Left just used a bunch of euphemisms to hide that.

It had many names in academia like critical theory and post-structuralism. It spawned gender and race studies and a plethora of other ways to categorize all that was wrong with America. In politics, it started under the mantle of liberalism, but they were more revolutionary than that. It morphed into progressivism which had many of the same goals, but more radical plans to get them done. It has been moving steadily leftward since then.

They began teaching these ideas to incoming cohorts of students. Many of whom stayed on and have become the progressively liberal faculty in our universities today. The irony is that as the shift leftward continued, many of yesterday's student-turned-liberal faculty have been marked as not liberal enough by today's students.

The natural state of youth is rebellion and they had ready recruits for a war to destroy the status quo. Their numbers grew and they began to push aside and replace the old guard of academia through attrition. The old professors who thought their jobs were teaching young people a rigorous understanding of particular disciplines and how to think rationally retired. The new ones who replaced them knew their job was not teaching students how to think, but what to think.

Indoctrination was the method and they took much of their doctrine from the Communist systems. They created a requirement for belief in their ideology punishable by rejection or banishment. They built a party cadre ready to spread the word and begin changing the world, starting with America.

They were smart about picking their battles, too. They began with some major issues that truly needed to be fixed: civil rights and equality for women. It's almost embarrassing to hear the current crop of activists howling about systemic racism and patriarchal oppression instead of recognizing the advances we've made. In the 1950s, those things were still a disgraceful stain and that needed to change.

They were deeply embedded in our culture and the fight to change them sometimes spilled over into protests and even riots. They were really the last major steps in the one hundred fifty plus-year journey to fulfill the promise of the Constitution that all men were created equal and must be treated accordingly.

They began to deploy student activists as the shock troops of change and they built private organizations dedicated to promoting the liberal/progressive agenda. They supported candidates who shared their worldview and a self-supporting system developed. The believers were trained in college and earned their spurs on the protest activism front then moved back into academia, non-profits, politics, and government.

Early on, they grasped the power of the bureaucracy and how it lasted even as elections changed the names at the top. The faceless administrators wielded the actual levers of power and they began filling those positions with their fellow travelers.

The truly brilliant aspect of this was how it allowed the liberal/progressive ideology to spread like a virus. The more they solidified control of academia the more pervasive these teachings became for all who passed though our universities. The professors got progressively more radical and the indoctrination spread from liberal arts programs to the hard sciences, engineering, and other fields of study.

This meant even those who didn't actively sign up to fight for the cause still got a solid grounding in the party propaganda. They took that with them after graduation regardless of what they went on to do. It ended the university system as an unbiased training ground for professionals and turned it into a place to get credentialed as a member of the liberal elite. It became a grounding in the right, meaning Left, ways to think about society.

THE MILITARY INDUSTRIAL COMPLEX

The analogue to this on the Right was a pipeline that turned out professionals fit for entering the corporate world or the burgeoning defense and intelligence machine.

The business of America has always been business. For those on the political Right, it was not just an acceptable endeavor, it was the preferred place for their children to aspire to. In the booming economic times following World War II, it was a path to prosperity and power.

The other conservative institution was our national security operations. The threat of two Communist superpowers required powerful U.S. capabilities. Our military and intelligence capabilities had to be robust and global in nature even in what was ostensibly peace time. The need for the best weapons and equipment led to a major expansion of the defense industry. The need to know what our enemies were up to did the same for our intelligence gathering capabilities.

The reason for this was easily evident in the expansionist nature of our enemies, especially the Soviet Union. The alliance of convenience and necessity we had with them during World War II ended very quickly. It turned into a head to head competition for global dominance and control. This became the Cold War and a struggle not just of major powers, but of Western Democracy against Communism.

Similar to the Left, this combined universe of career paths for members of the Right also coalesced into a self-supporting establishment of like minded people—the national security apparatus safeguarding the American way and the business contingent keeping the engines of growth and prosperity rolling along.

THE AMERICAN INTERNAL COLD WAR

As the two opposing forces in America built their empires at home, they increasingly began to maneuver against each other. They also began to settle into what felt like an agreeable stalemate.

This went along in comfortable conflict until President Reagan (with great help from Britain's Prime Minister, Margaret Thatcher, and

Pope John Paul II) defeated the Soviet Union. As undeniably good as that was for the entire world, it removed the very raison d'être for many Conservatives. Fighting communism was a noble vocation and without it the massive array of institutions devoted to winning the Cold War were without a guiding mission.

Of course, it was not a mistake to defeat the Soviets, but it made the Right vulnerable to attack at home from the Left. The fall of the Berlin Wall led to what the Left began to call the Peace Dividend. They had plenty of places where they were ready to spend it. They saw the entire edifice Conservatives had constructed as a perfect place to begin redistributing wealth. A popular bumper sticker of the time read:

"It will be a great day when our schools get all the money they need and the Pentagon has to hold a bake sale to buy a bomber."

It also made the traditional career path in national security for conservative youth less appealing. There was a giddy and ultimately unwarranted belief the world had become a safer place and the Right was no longer needed to keep us all safe from nuclear Armageddon or other dangers.

This coincided with the near total control of academia by the Left. When anti-Communism was a guiding ideology there was a sort of immunity for Conservatives while in college. The feeling was, "Of course, there's this silly socialism and communist-lite stuff going around but we can laugh it off because the real threat is still so deadly obvious." Once that shared sense of threat dissipated, the immunity departed along with it. Now conservatives were just as much the targets of indoctrination and the camaraderie of fellow anti-communists to help them resist it had disappeared.

Over the following decades, the "education" received at universities included increasing doses of liberal guilt and progressive ideology. It increased the percentage of liberals in professional positions as well. The educated class in America was moving well to the Left of the general population.

The end of the external Cold War opened another front for the Left in the American internal Cold War and they began to chip away at the military industrial complex. While the Right had built the national security establishment that gave them both job security and a purpose, the Left had always opposed those efforts with varying degrees of success. Now the main enemy was gone and the Republican establishment was floundering to justify its existence.

President George H.W. Bush was a weak and rudderless leader, especially after such a towering figure as President Reagan. Even though the actual fall of the Berlin Wall happened during Bush's presidency, he received little credit for it. Without the need for the institutions of the Right to safeguard us against an existential threat like the Soviet Union, there was no real selling point for Republicans. That became painfully obvious in the 1992 presidential election as Bill Clinton wiped the floor with Bush 41.

THE LAST MODERATE DEMOCRAT AND
THE RISE OF THE NEOCONS

The next eight years showed the loss of focus for the Republican establishment and President Clinton made tremendous inroads advancing the liberal agenda. The only saving grace was that he was a relatively moderate Democrat compared to what was coming down the pike. But still, every step to the Left made future degradation that much easier.

The real losses in the internal Cold War during the Clinton years were in the eroding of our cultural, moral and ethical values. Bill was a likeable rogue to many and certainly an excellent politician. He was also a serial adulterer and both he and his wife, Hillary, seemed corrupt and unsavory to many. President John F. Kennedy had been just as much of a philanderer but the public perception of his Administration was still Camelot and the beautiful people, a sort of American royalty.

Bill and Hillary created no such atmosphere and the lower moral standard they set was matched in our culture. Loose liberal values replaced enforcing morality and personal responsibility with a "do what feels good" mentality. TV and movies increasingly became avenues for propagation of the liberal and progressive worldview. This period of the late 1980s through the 1990s was the final iteration of the slow, steady, and very successful movement to the Left that had been underway since the 1950s.

The pendulum swing of American politics gave President George W. Bush the chance to defeat President Clinton's former Vice President, Al Gore, in the 2000 election. Bush benefitted from the Clinton scandal fatigue and also the general smarmy, unlikeable nature of Gore. Even so, the election still came down to a drawn out set of recounts, the introduction of "hanging chads," and eventually a Supreme Court ruling.

Bush 43 was the perfect example of an establishment Republican. He was packaged to look appealing in an era of relative prosperity with no major enemies or national security threats.

Karl Rove, a senior advisor and Deputy Chief of Staff, marketed him as a "Compassionate Conservative" which is as close to just admitting you're Democrat Lite as we may ever see. They used it to get W into the White House. Once there, he was the first Republican President in modern times forced to compete in our internal Cold War on the Democrats chosen battlefield of domestic policy.

He happily continued the preferred strategy of the Republican establishment which was lose as slowly as possible and under no circumstances fight as hard or dirty as your opponents. The concern always seemed to be "What would the other members of the country club think?"

Until 9/11.

That cataclysmic catastrophe returned the raison d'être of the American Right. We had a viable enemy again and they had just struck our homeland in a way no enemy had ever done. Amidst the heartbreak and horror came a return to steely resolve and President Bush became the leader of a revitalized national security and intelligence machine. It even spawned the largest bureaucratic move ever made, adding a Department of Homeland Security to the institutions of the Right.

Even though the Right had owned and operated the machinery of intelligence and war since World War II, it had not always covered itself in glory. Victory over the Soviet Union without ever rolling tanks or flying nuclear missiles was an amazing achievement. And one that could be claimed by the combined efforts of the two strongholds of the Right, national security and business.

We never had to fight the Soviets because we broke the Communist system by forcing them to try and keep up with our defense and business output. They used totalitarian control to try and make a creaky, inefficient system compete with the most powerful economy and defense conglomerate ever. They didn't stand a chance.

The rest of our military exploits in the post WWII era were unimpressive; and poorly conceived and executed. The Korean war (1950-1953) was a proxy war with China we had to join directly to stop a total defeat and even then we ended up with a tie. The war in Vietnam (1955-1975) was a bad idea that took two decades and 58,220 American casualties to figure out was a loss. The invasions into Grenada (1983) and Panama (1989) did not quality as war though they are technically victories. Operation Desert Storm (1991) had the scale of a war and was a crushing defeat for the expansionist goals of Iraqi Dictator Saddam Hussein. But, it also left a wounded tyrant in power.

The war machine run by the Right too closely resembled the political machine run by country club Republicans. They were both designed to win if possible. But if things got tough, to not lose, or to lose graciously and without taking extreme measures to fight and win. It was a version of the British concept "That's just not cricket, old chap."

The terrorist attack on our soil September 11, 2001, galvanized the nation and the world. America was now the leader of the free world again as we fought back against barbaric monsters. Out of tragedy was born the most fortuitous circumstances for a Commander in Chief. He got to take the fight to a common enemy shared by Americans and our friends. Team Right was back in charge and the military industrial intelligence complex was in full action mode.

The team that President Bush put into play were known as neocons from the Neoconservative movement. It was built by former liberals who were hawkish on foreign policy and couldn't stomach the leftward lurch of their party. They believed the proper application of American power could solve just about any problem. We were about to get a chance to see if they were correct.

The initial counterattack went brilliantly. A partnership with the Northern Alliance in Afghanistan allowed a small collection of U.S. Special Forces and U.S. precision strike capabilities to defeat the Taliban in short order. Their government fell and the state that allowed al Qaeda, which literally means "the base," to have a home base was gone.

But we didn't get Osama bin Laden and that along with a misguided belief we could turn Afghanistan into a functioning country led President Bush and his neocon advisers to a massive mistake: They decided to stay, and worse, began nation-building.

Afghanistan has long been deemed the graveyard of empires. Alexander the Great, the British, and the Soviets all went there and failed. America would learn that same painful lesson. The hellish terrain and hellbent tribes of Afghanistan cannot be tamed. Twenty years later, we still haven't managed to extricate ourselves from a war we will not win.

This is a loss we just haven't put on the board yet. The responsibility for all the lives lost since those first months lies on the neocon war machine. They were never willing to fight hard and ugly enough to win nor were they willing to look at the reality of defeat and cut our losses.

Unfortunately, that wasn't the only act of hubris and poor execution President Bush had in store for us. He spent the rest of the goodwill the world had bestowed on an America wounded by 9/11 on a plan to invade Iraq and rid Saddam of his weapons of mass destruction (WMD).

There is a lot of revisionist history from the Left saying everyone knew Saddam had no WMD. That's largely a lie as the U.S. and almost all the allied intelligence agencies agreed he did have them. Even Democrats including Nancy Pelosi (D-CA)[7] and Barack Obama agreed about Saddam having WMD.

Now let me be clear—I suffer no illusions about Saddam Hussein. He is a brutal man. A ruthless man. A man who butchers his own people to secure his own power. He has repeatedly defied UN resolutions, thwarted UN inspection teams, developed chemical and biological weapons, and coveted nuclear capacity. He's a bad guy. The world, and the Iraqi people, would be better off without him.

—STATE SENATOR BARACK OBAMA (DEMOCRAT, ILLINOIS) SPEECH

AT FEDERAL PLAZA, CHICAGO, ILLINOIS OCTOBER 2, 2002[8]

The problem was, they were all badly wrong.

Saddam did have chemical weapons and he had used them in 1988 against the Kurds in Iraq. This was a verified fact. By the time President Bush was ready to take him out, however, he had little to no real capabilities at all. He certainly didn't have the nuclear and biological programs that the Bush Administration told the world he did.

Similar to Afghanistan, the initial phase of Operation Iraqi Freedom went very well. The Thunder Run to Baghdad toppled Saddam's regime and he slunk off to his hometown to hide. Just like in Afghanistan, we didn't capture the ringleader and we began another attempt at nation-building.

To be fair and accurate, Iraq actually was a nation unlike Afghanistan, which was only a collection of warring tribes in a region where someone drew lines on a map. The people of Iraq were educated, had civic institutions, and a viable government. We had just freed them from the rule of a tyrannical despot who came from a minority group in the population. He had only maintained control through pure, ruthless evil and oppression.

It was possible and even reasonable to expect that a nation of some sort could emerge that was at least not hostile to the United States. That required competent help from the country that just vanquished Saddam's regime. The nation-building machine of the Right was terribly short of the strategy or skills needed to pull that off. What followed was a cavalcade of bad decisions poorly executed. They led us from an easy victory to a deadly, slogging war.

The first and most unforgiveable error was disbanding the Iraqi military and sending trained fighters back home with no way to feed their families. Saddam's forces were evil and their main skill had been oppressing their own people. But they were the only thing that had kept the peace. Now his former troops were stripped of weapons, power, and honor; and were booted out with no prospects and a healthy hatred of the United States.

Of course, they formed an insurgency to fight us. What other choice did they have? And they were good at it. It was a direct match for their skill set which was striking fear into the heart of the populace to gain compliance. They used it to get a foothold in their tribal regions where, as Chinese dictator Chairman Mao noted, a guerrilla moves among the people as a fish swims in the sea. They did this and the people either supported them or were scared to oppose them.

Saddam's former troops, now turned insurgents, wreaked havoc among the occupying U.S. forces, and since we had disbanded the Iraqi Army we had no local knowledge or forces able to help us turn the tide among the populace. We were losing the war and the death toll of our troops was enormous. Their preferred technique was hitting us with improvised explosives rather than taking on our far superior firepower in force-on-force confrontations. Eventually a splinter group called al Qaeda in Iraq formed. Far from actually defeating our terrorist enemy in Afghanistan, we had literally created the conditions that caused our enemies to grow and proliferate in Iraq.

The cadres from the national security organs of the Right whom we sent to build and administer a new Iraq were hopelessly inadequate to the task. First, few had the necessary language skills or area expertise; and second, there was no institutional knowledge of nation-building since the last time we did it was the Marshall Plan in Germany after America was victorious in World War II. They floundered and failed in Iraq. It often seemed their main function was helping the defense contractors burn truckloads of $100 bills.

Fortunately, we had a few mavericks in the military who actually knew what an insurgency was and understood the strategy and tactics needed to defeat one. They convinced President Bush to order the Surge in 2007 which provided a sufficient number of troops to fill the void left by the Iraqi Army. Our strategy then changed to Counterinsurgency, or COIN. This meant sending a large force into enemy controlled territory and using them to protect the local populace from the insurgents. It was a completely different type of warfare than rolling tanks and just taking out bad guys with massively superior firepower. And it worked.

This was essential for winning the hearts and minds of the people. It was a dangerous mission since it meant leaving the relative safety and security of the big bases and living side by side with the locals. It was the only way to gain their trust. As we pacified areas, we could provide work for the military-aged males securing their villages and families. This broke the back of the insurgency once the people had skin in the game and a way to work for a better life.

Real elections were held and a new Iraqi government was formed. The Iraq War was costly and a long grind, but it was eventually a victory. The problem was it showed the world the inability of the great American engine of power to function efficiently or effectively. The Right had now massively increased the scope and scale of its institutional might, but had become a large, lumbering beast that broke as many things as it fixed.

The goodwill America had been gifted after 9/11 was used up. The war in Iraq and the continuing one in Afghanistan caused many problems with our allies and others around the world.

The Global War on Terror was not doing much better. Osama bin Laden was still free despite President Bush's promises to "bring the terrorists to justice." The only justice terrorists saw was being killed on the battlefield. The U.S. detention camp at Guantanamo Bay had a bunch of al Qaeda bad guys stashed there and the CIA operated black sites to extract intelligence from others we caught. Unfortunately, little actionable intelligence was gained and none of the bad guys at Gitmo were successfully tried or executed. In many cases, they were released or traded back to their terrorist homelands.

It was another failure of the institutional Right to deliver on the core mission of keeping America safe and defeating our enemies. The inability of President Bush to gain a single conviction in military tribunals is a dismal failure that showed the fecklessness of the establishment team and tactics. Khalid Sheikh Mohammed, a lead al Qaeda planner of 9/11, still sits in Gitmo to this day getting fat on American taxpayer dollars.

Since 9/11, we have failed to bring nearly any terrorists to justice, failed to win the war to take away their safe haven in Afghanistan, and allowed al Qaeda to survive and even grow. We started a war in Iraq based on bad intelligence and fought it unwisely. Even in the end when we defeated the insurgency, we failed to gain an agreement to stay and help midwife that fragile new democracy. That mistake created the conditions that eventually led to the rise of ISIS.

Not really much of a record to brag about.

The Left was fighting a bit uphill when Bush was President due to the initial widespread support for retaliatory actions from 9/11. But their culture and academia armies were still very busy. Dislike, even hatred, of Bush united the Left, energizing them to continue chipping away at traditional culture and values. By the end of President George W. Bush's two terms, The Right was in one of the least advantageous positions in the internal Cold War with the Left since its inception.

PART II

THE AMERICAN COLD WAR

HEATS UP (2009-2020)

BOTTOM LINE UP FRONT
America is now fighting a second Civil War. Extremists on both ends of the political spectrum are an active danger. BLM/Antifa calls the government of the United States evil and think it must be replaced by any means necessary. The far Right has a contingent that is just as anti-government as some of the anarchists. Let's hope the rest of the country can reject vitriolic rhetoric and violent actions. We need to collectively deescalate and consolidate based on the one unifying American value that at least there should be an America. It is by no means guaranteed.

The polarized nature of our politics and culture has led us to this point. There are bad people on both sides, but none of the extremists have the high ground or legitimate cause to unleash the violence we have already seen. There are peaceful means to solve these grievances and we need to make a commitment to using the strong legal and civil structures that hold this country together. First priority should be avoiding a repeat of the one time we failed as a nation to do that. There was horrific bloodshed and close to a million lives were lost in our first Civil War.

Both political and militant actions moved us from the Cold War with the USSR to violence in the streets of America. We'll examine the spectrum of extra-political action from peaceful protests through armed insurrection. Our Founders ensured the Constitution of the United States contained the means to oppose domestic oppression. They had the forethought that we might someday again be faced with a tyranny that would require revolutionary force to depose.

The goal here is to absorb all of this and pull everyone we can back from the brink.

2

THE WARFARE OF POLITICS

PRESIDENT BARACK OBAMA could have brought about unity as the first Black President. Instead, he set about systematically empowering the activist groups on the Left. He became the divider and said corrosive things that inflamed racial tensions like "The police acted stupidly" and "If I had a son he'd look like Trayvon Martin." The guy with the bully pulpit certainly seemed to be aligning himself on the side of those pitching grievances. His validation launched the Social Justice Warriors as the shock troops of the Left.

The slow march toward Socialism picked up steam on his watch and Americans began to notice and get angry. The Left claimed this was racism, but it was really just a realization that the fundamental values of this country were under attack. Gender absurdity, open Borders, racial grievances, climate capitulation, and a host of other leftist causes were absorbed under the banner of Wokeness, the new brand for Socialism.

Climate Hysteria is a perfect example. Look at Greta Thunberg, the Swedish teenager internationally lauded as the person to listen to on the environment. Failure to join in her crusade to rid us of cows and cars means you are personally killing the planet and all its inhabitants. Calls for tolerance of the ever-increasing LGBTQABCDEFG acronym include the concept that words are violence. This means that "misgendering" someone—that is, calling them by a pronoun they do not identify with—is the same as physically assaulting them.

The fanatics were increasingly setting the agenda for the mainstream Democrats. They were forcing the whole party to follow their path to righteousness because crossing them would lead to your destruction. They became the enforcers for an extreme secular religious sect akin to the brown/blackshirts of earlier totalitarian political movements.

That's how they treat their own. Imagine, or just watch at the riots, the hatred for the heretics defined as anyone on the Right. We were no longer political opponents with different policy ideas to be debated. We were evil incarnate to be exposed and expelled from the public square. That's not an exaggeration as prominent Democrats have called for public consequences for Trump supporters.

Robert Reich, Labor Department secretary under President Bill Clinton and adviser to President Barack Obama, tweeted:

When this nightmare is over, we need a Truth and Reconciliation Commission…It would erase Trump's lies, comfort those who have been harmed by his hatefulness, and name every official, politician, executive, and media mogul whose greed and cowardice enabled this catastrophe.[9]

MSNBC host Chris Hayes was also on board with treating political opponents as war criminals:

The most humane and reasonable way to deal with all these people, if we survive this, is some kind of truth and reconciliation commission.[10]

PRESIDENT OBAMA DIVIDED AMERICA

The turn from the American internal Cold War to the current Second Civil War began on President Obama's watch.

In 2008, Republicans sent a relic of the Cold War, Senator John McCain (R-AZ), to the presidential campaign trail. He was the best they had to offer to defend their far from stellar record after eight years of President George W. Bush. McCain was up against the Left's newly-minted messiah, Barack Obama. It was a wipeout. The political pendulum effect was swinging away from eight years of a Republican administration. A massive economic collapse didn't help much either.

Obama was so many things for the Left: a historic first Black President, a moderate-sounding radical, and a bright, likeable politician. He also benefitted from the massive crush the entire media had over him. These were the days when formerly hardball MSNBC anchor Chris Matthews said after an Obama speech, "I felt a thrill going up my leg." He was touted as "The One," "The Messiah," the bringer of Democrat dreams.

With Obama as the smiling, affable frontman, the Left seized the opportunity to advance on all fronts in the American Cold War. Obama himself had even said the quiet thing out loud during the 2008 election.

We are five days away from fundamentally transforming the United States of America.[11]

As opposed to a thrill up our legs, that sent a chill down the spines of many patriotic Americans. We rightly saw this was a direct assault on the foundations of our country. It sparked the first real populist movement of the modern era, the Tea Party, in early 2009.

Taxed Enough Already (TEA) was a reaction to the inevitable push by Obama and the Left to do some wealth redistribution. You can't do any good socialism until you have piles of other people's money to play with. The Tea Party saw a collection of massive spending programs on the horizon and they knew even though we have presses we can't just print free money. Citizens flocked to stand up against the free-spending Democrats.

The Tea Party was a collection of likeminded patriots with no real central headquarters or organization. It was a spontaneous emergence of the fighting wing of the Right in revolt against the weakness of the party establishment. For too long, they had seen Republican candidates run as conservatives, but once they got to Washington it was go along, get along and don't rock the boat. The Tea party wanted the boat rocked and the tea and potentially the Republican leadership tossed into the harbor.

President Obama and the Democrats went right to work on one of the biggest Leftist dreams: Socialized medicine. It took almost to the midterm elections to do it and in the end, they rammed ObamaCare through without a single Republican vote. This was a huge Democrat victory for fundamental transformation but it also served to stir up recruitment on the Right. The enemy was more obvious now and they had to be stopped.

The 2010 midterm elections were a red wave wipeout of the Dems this time. Republicans picked up seven seats in the Senate and 63 seats in the House. This was the largest shift since 1948. The American internal Cold War was heating up.

The Right and Left had been drifting apart steadily in all aspects of life for decades. There was, however, still a sense that we all shared a love for this country even as we differed in how to run things. President Obama had grudges that led him to begin challenging that. His fundamental transformation required tearing down many of our institutions and principles.

The Obama Administration empowered Leftist non-profits, funded whacked-out new degree programs dreamed up by academia, and hung out with the celebrities and Hollywood types who shared his views. They all believed America was a failed state in desperate need of a reboot.

Obama was the perfect output of the radicalized university system the Left had built. He cut his teeth on Marxism and Critical Race Theory and although he was smart enough to campaign as a moderate, the radical Left was where his heart was. He had a lot of political capital as the first Black President even though members of his own party treated him as something of a token during the campaign.

Senate Majority Leader Harry Reid (D-NV) noted Obama's "light-skinned" appearance and speaking style "with no Negro dialect, unless he wanted to have one."[12]

Even his eventual running mate Joe Biden said:

I mean, you got the first mainstream African-American who is articulate and bright and clean and a nice-looking guy.[13]

He came into office with a chip on his shoulder and the means to do something about it. He learned the America-hating ropes in college. Then he honed his skills playing the community organizer game in Chicago.

Once Obama began operating as the Activist in Chief, the Left also began framing any opposition to him as racist in nature. That was a huge advantage since it armored him against many perfectly valid complaints. It also helped him claim the racial divide in America was a bigger problem than it actually was.

One of the most divisive and antagonistic things he did was to weaponize the activist groups on the Left, especially the ones focused on racial issues. He validated the concept of social justice warriors by personally injecting himself into several high-profile race-related issues.

Henry Louis Gates, a Black professor at Harvard, was arrested for disorderly conduct when police found him breaking into a house in July 2009. It was his own house, but the police didn't know who he was when they responded to a neighbor's 911 call. He became belligerent and refused to provide identification. He berated the police accusing them of only hassling him because he was Black. He was released after his identity was confirmed and the charges were dropped. Gates took to the airwaves claiming this was evidence of systemic racism and the media saw an opportunity to push a wedge issue, so they played it up.

Obama did too when he made a statement claiming "the police acted stupidly." This was a major use of his position as President to rouse racial tensions over an incident that was hardly worthy of the attention. But it had supposed racial discrimination toward a Harvard professor, a Harvard professor mind you, so it was cat nip to the media and activists.

Later in his Presidency, Obama threw more gas on the fire commenting on the shooting death of Trayvon Martin, a 17-year-old Black kid shot and killed in a fight with a man named George Zimmerman in 2012. This was portrayed as a racially-motivated murder of an innocent child simply coming back from buying a bag of Skittles. The narrative was Trayvon was shot for the crime of being Black.

To make it seem more racist-y, the media invented the term White Hispanic to describe the shooter Zimmerman, whose mother was Hispanic. They needed to get the word White into play or this was just violence between a Black kid and a Latino. It also helped draw attention away from the fact there were wounds on Zimmerman's head. Those corroborated his story that Martin had been beating his head against the pavement and he fired in self-defense.

There was outrage and protests galore. While the investigation into the incident was still ongoing, President Obama took the opportunity again to make sure it was framed as a racial issue by saying, "If I had a son, he'd look like Trayvon."[14]

When Obama piled on to these issues, he lit the first match and launched the movement that led directly to the conflagration of the 2020 riots. He gave the social justice warriors the Presidential Seal of Approval. The Left now had its foot soldiers.

The response to Obama from the Right was widespread dislike and disagreement with his administration and its policies. It never coalesced into an understanding that he was leading the vanguard of a broader and more dangerous revolutionary movement. In some ways the Right, just like the Left, was caught up in the view of Obama as a celebrity. That led to more opposition toward the person creating a blindness to the hordes of activists coming up from behind him.

The media painted all of this as racist White people feeling their country slipping away from them because of the Black man in power. But it wasn't that, it was his policies not his color. He was dividing us by winding up the race baiters and grievance culture on the Left.

Perceptions of negative racial relations actually increased during the Obama Presidency. A poll near the end of his second term confirmed this with 54% of Americans saying race relations got worse under Obama.[15] He had the chance as the first Black President to be a uniter, but he went the opposite direction. He told Black people they were still oppressed, the police were their enemy, and the simple fact of being Black could get you killed.

Black Lives Matter (BLM) became the rallying cry and that group formed after the Trayvon Martin death. It grew larger in 2014 when another young Black man, Michael Brown, was killed by a police officer in St. Louis. This incident touched off protests that turned into riots and BLM was at the forefront.

Both the Trayvon Martin and Michael Brown incidents shared common threads. The victim was portrayed as a young innocent singled out and slain only for the color of his skin. The narrative was untrue in both cases.

As noted, Trayvon Martin was beating George Zimmerman's head against the pavement. The Michael Brown case had the media calling him a gentle giant and using a picture of him in his graduation cap and gown. The false claim that he was shot with his hands up prompted a nationwide deluge of celebrities and media personalities play acting with their hands in the air saying, "Hands up, don't shoot."[16]

The reality was much different and they steadfastly ignored video showing Michael Brown conducting a strong-arm robbery of a convenience store and violently tossing the owner around like a rag doll. The hands-up tale was a fantasy. Evidence and witness statements showed Brown had approached the police car after being told multiple times to stop. He reached inside the car and struggled with the officer who shot him in self-defense.

None of this mattered to the social justice crowd. They and the media were running a propaganda campaign. They wanted to convince the American people that the current state of our country for Blacks might as well be Selma, Alabama in 1965.

There was a large cadre of university-trained activists who were ready to carry the banners and storm the barricades. Critical Race Theory had informed them America is a White Supremacist country. That Systemic Racism oppresses Black people and all White people are beneficiaries and therefore racist. It is a grotesque mockery of the reality in the country. But you can't tell that to the true believers and they wanted retribution and reparations.

The biggest problem for the Right is a complete lack of any mechanisms, institutions or ability to fight back against this in any meaningful way. All our energy had gone into building a national security and business backbone. We were basically unarmed in this battle. The Left knew it and smelled blood.

The protests got larger every time there was a questionable killing by police. There are certainly times when the police overstep and even commit crimes up to and including murder. The Black Lives Matter crowd didn't care whether the shooting was justified. If police killed a Black person, the fight was on.

On the global front, it's not like the vaunted national security apparatus of the Right did much good during the Obama years either. They managed to let him make the single worst foreign policy agreement in the country's history—The Iran Deal. Republicans controlled the Senate which has a Constitutional authority to advise and consent on treaties. They never even managed to use that to force a meaningful vote. Obama and crew lied to the country, and no one even saw the final version or the secret side deals they negotiated.

The Obama team put us into a nuclear deal that only let us inspect where they allowed us to and expired in a dozen years. At that point, the Iranian nuke program would have been actually legal and could have operated with no international supervision. To top it all off, the

Mullahs were sent a plane filled with pallets of cash, half a billion dollars, in the middle of the night.

President Obama bet on the wrong pony at the racetrack: He kept us at war in Afghanistan but pulled our forces out of Iraq. He created a vacuum that was filled by Iran and the birth of ISIS from the ashes of al Qaeda in Iraq, which we had defeated. Hundreds of thousands of people in the Middle East would die for this failure. Obama reinforced the war we had already lost in Afghanistan and cut and ran from the war we won in Iraq by failing to secure the peace.

The Obama foreign policy echoed his belief that America was a failed state with plenty to apologize for. He ran around the globe in a posture of cringing capitulation. He proved he didn't understand the concept of or believe in American exceptionalism when he said:

> I believe in American exceptionalism, just as I suspect that the Brits believe in British exceptionalism and the Greeks believe in Greek exceptionalism.[17]

That is not just a sad misunderstanding of America's importance to the world as the sole superpower. He didn't even get the meaning right. American exceptionalism means we were the first nation conceived in the idea that the state is subordinate to the individual. It's a statement about liberty not about national pride. President Obama was wrong on both counts.

He did not want an exceptional America of any kind, he wanted an America that was just one nation among many. A good member of the global community, basically France with more people…and the Grand Canyon. And he spent his Presidency trying to make us subordinate to as many transnational organizations and treaties as he could.

The Paris Climate Accords was a perfect example and a way to empower the climate hysterics while forcing the corporate powers in line. It was also another treaty that the Senate failed to gain any advice or consent authority over. It shackled the U.S. economy to carbon reduction goals that did not apply to the world's super polluter Communist China. They produce one third of all the carbon in the world, but they and India skated free while we were supposed to bear the pain.

Obama was a very successful Second Civil War time President from the perspective of the Left. He weakened America abroad and managed to open a new front against the Right with BLM where we are the weakest. He took the Left to their strongest position and victory seemed to be in sight.

All they needed was for him to pass the field marshal baton to Hillary Clinton during the 2016 presidential election and finish off the Right. Total demolition was near. She would deliver a fully socialism-compliant, faux democracy where we could vote for any candidate they chose.

Imagine for a moment a Hillary Clinton inauguration in 2017. Now stop howling and let's consider what that would have meant. Immediately filling the empty seat on the Supreme Court left by the death of Justice Antonin Scalia in 2016 with another Constitutional revisionist like Supreme Court Justices Sonia Sotomayor and Elena Kagan. Then another in 2018 to replace Justice Anthony Kennedy and a third in 2020 for Justice Ruth Bader Ginsburg.

That would have replaced a 4-4 split of Conservatives and Liberals on her first day with a 6-3 liberal advantage and that's counting Chief Justice Roberts as a conservative, which probably isn't warranted.

It is not extreme to say that would have been a grave and mortal danger to this Republic. How easy for them to decide the First Amendment doesn't pertain to hate speech, or that establishment of religion means you may go to church, but your daily life will be subject to secular oversight. Let there be no doubt the Second Amendment would have been an early casualty. Perhaps the right to keep and bear muskets might have survived but nothing much beyond that.

We really dodged a bullet when Hillary went down in flames.

THEN CAME TRUMP

The silent majority had been awakened and they were mad about the weak Republicans who campaigned as Conservatives yet governed as Democrats. Trump brought a fighting spirit that called them out. No more would we simply lose to the Left slowly, we needed to win. That attitude and message resonated on both the Right and the Left for completely different reasons.

When Trump was elected, the Left lost it. He was their worst nightmare. He was an unrepentant America First populist who didn't care what they thought or said about him. The Left began a four-year national tantrum and attempt to subvert and destroy him. No tactics were off limits and while the members of the permanent bureaucracy, known as Deep State, handled the internal undermining, the media ran full on propaganda efforts, and the Woke Mob took to the streets. President Trump made them so unhinged they ripped their masks off and screamed, "You're damn right we hate this country and we're going to burn it down and build a new one."

The Left was quite open about their desire to rid the country of the evil of Trump. They immediately branded their efforts as "The Resistance." It was a weak attempt to ride the coattails for the French Resistance from World War II who fought the Nazis. This dovetailed nicely with their constant smears of President Trump and basically anyone to the Right of Senator Bernie Sanders (D-VT) as Nazis.

They also had the Antifa goons who made an even weaker claim to be fighting fascists and loved to pass around cartoons online with the slogan "Punch A Nazi." The irony was the Antifa/BLM Mob had morphed into a functional equivalent of fascist Black Shirts. They attacked their political enemies and served to intimidate or hurt those on their side who failed to toe the party line.

The 2020 Riots were an outgrowth of that fueled by exaggerated tales of systemic racism by the police and the COVID-19 quarantines. The Woke Mob of Antifa and Black Lives Matter burned, looted, and even killed in their orgy of lawlessness and destruction. They were successful in scaring Democrat-run cities into compliance with their demands and the media ran cover for their "peaceful protests."

It turned into violent insurrection and domestic terrorism. Law enforcement was forced to cede territory to them in far too many places. When normal Americans saw this, they were appalled and many were now afraid. This led to groups on the Right standing up in opposition to the mob and we had confrontations and multiple killings as a result.

As angry as President Trump made the Left, they were destined to get a full four years of him. Let's look at what that meant and what he brought to the Right.

THE TRUMP DOCTRINE

Donald Trump ran for President in 2016 on the theme Make America Great Again. This was basically an acknowledgment that the actions of the Left and the weakness of the establishment Right had led America far astray. He was right and he reinvigorated the Right and gave it a fighting spirit that had been sorely lacking.

The specifics involved controlling our borders, removing regulations that stifle industry, revamping the tax code, renegotiating bad trade agreements, and getting us out of the endless wars overseas. All of these were very core conservative issues that had been discussed for many election cycles. But never delivered.

That was the difference supporters saw, a willingness to actually fight for these things once elected. Not just campaign like a warrior and govern like a milquetoast. The Trump Presidency would show he meant to fight for what he believed in and deliver what he had promised.

During his first two years, he accomplished a number of his political promises including the tax overhaul and removing massive numbers of government regulations that were stifling businesses. The pace of good policies led Rich Lowry, editor of *National Review,* which had devoted an entire issue to essays against Trump as the Republican nominee, to write a piece praising him:

> As the year ends, President Trump is compiling a solid record of accomplishment.[18]

President Trump took the U.S. out of the Paris Climate Accords which would have held us to economy-damaging standards without doing the same for China and India. He also ended our participation in the atrocious Iran Nuclear Deal which did not live up to the fantasy promises of the Obama Administration.

He was on a roll and all of this despite being subject to a Special Counsel investigation looking at allegations of collusion with Russia during the 2016 campaign. The Mueller Investigation became known by the White House and many on the Right as the Witch Hunt. It was based on a collection of shockingly thin connections of Trump associates to Russians. The only "evidence" was a dossier that was actually commissioned by the Hillary Clinton campaign during the 2016 presidential race as opposition research.

After the full investigation had run its course there was no evidence of collusion. Even worse, there ended up being a Justice Department investigation of the shameful partisan nature of the whole sordid attack on the Trump team by the Left. That eventually turned into its own Special Counsel which is still looking into criminal charges against those from the Obama Administration and some holdovers into Trump's term.

Another tactic of the Left was to demonize President Trump as a racist or supporter of White Supremacists. It began in earnest following the Charlottesville, Virginia protests in 2017 that ended with the murder of a counter-protestor by a vehicle ramming.

It was a rally of the radical Right to protest the destruction of Confederate statues and memorials. There were many unsavory groups including neo-Nazis, White supremacists, Antifa, and radical elements of the Left. Violent acts were committed by both sides. After the killing of Heather Heyer, who was not involved in any of that, President Trump spoke about the incident. He is often quoted inaccurately as saying there were "very fine people, on both sides" as if he were praising the neo-Nazis as simply very fine people.

What he actually said was:

...you had some very bad people in that group, but you also had people that were very fine people, on both sides.

That is already a different statement. He went further and specifically denounced the racist elements:

And you had people—and I'm not talking about the neo-Nazis and the white nationalists—because they should be condemned totally. But you had many people in that group other than neo-Nazis and white nationalists.[19]

This incident was in many ways the start of the current violence and this blatant misrepresentation of the President's response has been used as propaganda to fuel it.

An almost pathological need to bring Trump down infected much of the leadership of the Democrats and their media allies. They held hearings, leaked leaks, and kept digging and digging to find any pretext to attack him. They eventually came up with a particularly weak rationale that they spun up into his eventual impeachment and acquittal in the Senate.

It revolved around a phone call he had with the new leader of Ukraine. In it the President asked him to investigate ongoing allegations of corruption by former Vice President Joe Biden. The Democrat/Media complex thought they had him trying to influence a foreign government to dig up dirt on a potential political opponent for his reelection.

To do that they had to ignore the very real justification that if a sitting U.S. Vice President had been involved in corruption it was certainly worthy of investigation. President Trump had every right to request Ukraine examine those allegations. The Democrats and their media friends made the claim these allegations were disproven. In reality, the only debunking was done by Biden's political allies simply saying they were not true.

The story centered around Biden taking his son Hunter along with him on Air Force Two as Biden went on official trips for the Obama Administration. He allowed Hunter to conduct sales meetings for his consulting services in the countries they visited. This quite obviously showed prospective clients the connections he had to the top level of the U.S. government.

Hunter was highly unqualified for the business he sold in the Ukraine, getting himself a seat on the board of Burisma, an energy company. He scored this cushy $85k a month gig while his father was the lead for the Obama team on Ukraine policy. That is a grotesque conflict of interest right there just for starters. There was plenty more. The Left claimed it just didn't matter. Nothing to see here, move along.

The Democrats impeached President Trump in the House. They based this solely on the idea that he had no legitimate interest as President in finding out if Joe Biden had been using his office to enrich his family. The Senate promptly acquitted him but it was another unwarranted attack on the President. It showed the obsession the Left had and their willingness to try anything to take him down.

Interestingly, the issue of Hunter Biden came up again toward the end of the 2020 campaign. Again Joe Biden's supporters in the media came to his aid. A laptop owned by Hunter Biden was turned in by a computer store where he had left it for repairs. It contained massive amounts of truly bad things about Hunter personally and professionally. It showed drug use, prostitutes, and a degraded, decadent lifestyle. But more damagingly, it showed the extent of the business dealings and corruption he was involved with. It also pointed directly to his father, the Democrat nominee for President, Joe Biden.

This was immediately declared Russian disinformation by the Left's media outlets and Democrat talking heads. They got the story buried with this bogus claim. The social media companies literally hid it from view and banned the accounts of people who discussed it. It was a disgraceful example of actual collusion to affect an election.

That is now coming back to bite them as it was announced there are multiple investigations into the Biden family corruption by the Justice Department.

The Trump Presidency was a chaotic time due to all of these things as well as the nature of Trump himself to create and stir controversies. That paired with the media's obsessive desire to take him out led to constant stories taking pretty much everything he did and trying to generate outrage. Occasionally they were outrage worthy, but in the end they showed one of the main challenges faced by the Right: the media is no longer trying to pretend to be unbiased. They are the propaganda organ of the Left and will use their power to attack anyone on the Right who holds the wrong opinions.

President Trump made the biggest change to Republican politics since President Ronald Reagan. Much of the MAGA crowd had never engaged in politics at anywhere near this fervor before he entered the scene. They will not be going away and many will be taking more powerful positions in the hierarchy of the political Right.

The challenge will be getting both them and the establishment on the same sheet of music. If the 2020 election is any indicator, that is not going to be an easy one.

3

THE ELECTION INSURRECTION

THE 2020 PRESIDENTIAL ELECTION will go down as the most corrupt and damaging election in our Republic's history. The trust all Americans must have that every vote counts and only valid votes will be counted was breached. We must focus tremendous attention and energy on fixing that.

This will not be an exhaustive examination of all the problems with the election. It will focus on the actions by the Left that we failed to counter and now must deal with. We will also examine the actions and inactions of the Right that contributed to the failed outcome.

The attempts to challenge the 2020 presidential election were not our most shining moments. They reached a point of diminishing return and even became counterproductive. Unproven theories and accusations about voting machines, counterfeit ballots, and foreign interference spread so widely that the results will never be accepted by a significant number of Trump supporters. Those things are distracting from the gains Republicans made in the House and among minority voters overall.

Republicans lost the Senate runoff races in Georgia giving Democrats control of Congress and the Senate. This was partly due to some major supporters of President Trump telling people to stay home and not vote because of irregularities. The decision by Sen. Mitch McConnell (R-KY) to torpedo stimulus checks for people who have been financially devastated was another key factor. Continuing to focus on these issues can damage the momentum toward taking back the House of Representatives in 2022, which looks like a serious possibility.

That is not to say there were no irregularities, outright abuses, or even violations of the statutes and regulations that govern our elections. There were. Most of these egregious actions were done prior to the election by state and local officials with the express intent of ensuring more mail in ballots were accepted. Major steps to ensure the validity of mail in ballots were removed. This resulted in an anomalous decrease in rejected ballots.[20] This helped Biden and hurt Trump.

There are also huge numbers of invalid names on the voter rolls. This is unacceptable. We can't allow the Left to register any random person they can find who has a pulse and then keep large numbers of names on the rolls long after they no longer have one. It's a recipe for unaccountable ballots floating around. We saw that happen in this election.

Ballot harvesting is another unacceptable policy the Left has legally implemented in many places. This lets anyone go around gathering up absentee or mail in ballots and then deliver them to the polls as if they had been cast by the actual "voter." The Democrats have combined an uncontrolled registration process with the ability to mail out and gather ballots by third parties.

They can register homeless people or illegal aliens and then get ballots mailed out, sometimes to P.O. boxes they control. This was documented in previous elections in Orange County, California where dozens of people were registered to vote using a local dog park as their physical address. Others used a Starbucks or a city office building as their registered domicile. Many of these registrations had a mailing address in Sacramento all the way across the state.[21]

This opens the door for fraud and abuse. We cannot allow the combination of ballot harvesting and removal of strict identification and validity checks on these supposed votes to continue.

The time to challenge those policies and practices was prior to the election, not after a loss.

President Trump preloaded skepticism about mail in voting that prepped supporters to question it. The problem was that neither his campaign nor the Republican political machine did the legal ground work necessary to deal with the changes being made. In short, the Democrats made sure the country was awash in uncontrolled ballots and Republicans did nothing to prevent it.

The President was ill-served by the Republican National Committee (RNC) and his own campaign. Both failed to act and ensure that a fair election would be conducted. I was personally involved in providing both the RNC and the campaign leadership with detailed information about voting shenanigans in Orange County and the rest of California a year prior to the election.

Out of the $1.5B spent by the campaign and the $1B from the RNC, virtually none of that went to ensuring the Democrats plans to subvert the rules were stopped. Hundreds of 30 second ads produced by the establishment political parasite class were not going to overcome a deluge of uncontrolled ballots entering the system. But that is what they focused on.

We got outplayed.

Changing the laws and rules about voting at the state level is vital. That's where they are written and enforced. Ensuring fair elections must be a top priority. It's a critical first step on The Path to Victory.

The Democrat/media machine spent the entire Trump presidency attempting to delegitimize his win in 2016. This rightfully angered both Trump supporters and many mainstream citizens. The Left abused the power of the state to spy and investigate but found no crimes. That didn't stop the constant leaks and media amplification of their manufactured narrative that the Trump campaign conspired with the Russians to steal the election.

It was not at all difficult for many to believe the same forces conspired to swing the 2020 election against him. And they did.

The bias and censorship of the mainstream and social media outlets was shockingly obvious. The most egregious example was the quashing of the Hunter Biden laptop story.[22] There was so much information warfare against us it is difficult to catalog all of it.

The social media companies took the unprecedented step of becoming self-appointed arbiters of "The Truth." This essentially meant they labeled conservative ideas and opinions as false while promoting the people and positions of the Left. They began labeling President Trump's tweets as false or disputed. They did none of that to Biden or other Democrats.

They even banned major accounts from their platforms that discussed the Hunter Biden story in the weeks just prior to the election. Free speech anyone? The social media giants eventually had to backtrack on that, but not until after the damage was done. They hid a major scandal and claimed it was Russian disinformation. This is even more embarrassing now that it has been revealed there are multiple criminal investigations into Biden family corruption.

There was so much partisan tilting of the information playing field, it is reasonable to say the American people were denied the ability to make a fair and informed decision.

Concerns about the election began election night when FOX made a very early call saying Biden had won Arizona. This was long before any other outlet was even close to making that prediction. Then a number of the major swing states decided to shut down counting in the post-midnight time frame. This stopped them from getting enough ballots counted to be called either way.

President Trump was ahead in all of them, but the mail in ballots, which were strongly in favor of Joe Biden, were mostly still uncounted.

This led to an outcry on social media that the fix was in. That became louder when the next days showed the numbers for Biden eclipsing Trump and eventually all the media outlets called the election for him.

There were many theories about how the lead evaporated and the election overall was stolen. They included boxes of ballots being brought into polling places in the middle of the night, ballots were invalidated because voters were given Sharpies, or ballots kept under a table were counted after observers were sent home.

One of the largest focal points was the belief that voting machines from Dominion Systems had been used to systematically change votes for President Trump into votes for Joe Biden. Many different experts and a lot of non-experts weighed in on this. It gained steam as the best way to explain the large changes in vote reporting numbers.

All of these potential violations and a large number of affidavits from citizens and even some voting officials were taken up by both Trump campaign lawyers and some private lawyers. They produced a lot of lawsuits but none of them managed to invalidate or change the results in any of the swing states.

There were also groups organizing to protest against the election results. They represented a powerful social media presence and generated a large number of conservative followers. The problem was rallies and online agitating were not going to change facts on the ground.

No one proved in court that the voting machines were rigged or any other cases of wholesale fraud. The real problem was a failed set of institutions that make up the political Right. We got out-organized and out-maneuvered about the election rules before the fight began. Then we were abandoned by part of that establishment team once the challenges began.

The top law firms who had been happily cashing massive checks for business from the campaign refused to work on the election challenges.[23] They caved to pressure from Democrats and their media allies who organized efforts to attack their other clients. This left the President without the necessary expertise in the intricacies of election law to have even the slightest chance of prevailing in court.

Some of the losses were inevitable as state level courts ruled that policies, procedures, and practices that were in effect in previous elections could not be challenged. In Wisconsin, some rule violations made by the election commission had been in place since before 2016. That meant President Trump had won the state under the same rules that were now being challenged.

Even though a rule or practice violated a state law, you can't accept them when you win but not when you lose. They could have and should have been challenged prior to the 2020 vote. There was a flurry of rule-changing and emphasis on mail in and absentee voting largely driven by the COVID-19 crisis. The Democrats took full advantage and didn't let the crisis go to waste. They created an environment where it seemed anything vaguely resembling a ballot got included in the count.

It was much harder to get anything changed after the fact and the courts were very unfriendly. They gave no relief even when evidence showed the Election Commissions used rules that violated statutes in Wisconsin and the entire law expanding mail in voting in Pennsylvania ignored the State Constitution. The more these obvious transgressions were allowed to stand, the angrier people on the Right rightly became.

On 21 January, 2021, Joe Biden took the oath of office and became the 46th President of the United States. The question is what are the many people so invested in the stolen election scenario going to do?

Most will take their anger and put it where it belongs. They will vent on social media, neighborhood barbecues, and around the table at family get togethers. Many will not be satisfied with those outlets and they are not an insignificant number. They will refuse to accept the legitimacy of a Biden presidency and will want to take action. Some will undoubtedly go too far.

Some people pushed the idea of President Trump instituting martial law to change the results. That idea received immediate disdain as it should have. Unfortunately, it also got cheers from a large contingent. Those folks were deeply invested in overturning by any means necessary what they called a fraudulent and stolen election.

Trump was never going to try the martial law gambit. For one thing, there is virtually zero chance the military would have agreed. They are required to refuse unlawful orders, which this would have been. This translated into growing frustration among the disaffected and increased the likelihood of violent responses such as the storming of the Capitol.

We saw the first instance of that on January 6, 2021, when Congress met to count and accept the votes of the Electoral College. There were already rallies and protests planned and President Trump called on supporters to come to DC. The publicized goal was to get Vice President Mike Pence and Republicans in Congress to somehow stop the acceptance of the vote. It was basically the last formal hurdle prior to Inauguration Day.

It was destined to fail as it would require Democrats to vote against the Electoral College results. That was never going to happen and there was no magic bullet Pence could fire as presiding official to stop it. Nor should he have. People are rightfully angry about improprieties in how the election was conducted, but that does not mean the Vice President should invent an extra-Constitutional power to veto the Electoral votes from the states. Two wrongs don't make a right.

There were a number of Republican Senators and Congressmen who had publicly stated their intentions to protest the results and force a vote on its legitimacy. Senator Ted Cruz (R-TX) was joined by many of them in a letter which stated their objections.

> The election of 2020, like the election of 2016, was hard fought and, in many swing states, narrowly decided. The 2020 election, however, featured unprecedented allegations of voter fraud, violations and lax enforcement of election law, and other voting irregularities…
>
> Voter fraud has posed a persistent challenge in our elections, although its breadth and scope are disputed. By any measure, the allegations of fraud and irregularities in the 2020 election exceed any in our lifetimes…

Ideally, the courts would have heard evidence and resolved these claims of serious election fraud. Twice, the Supreme Court had the opportunity to do so; twice, the Court declined...

To wit, Congress should immediately appoint an Electoral Commission, with full investigatory and fact-finding authority, to conduct an emergency 10-day audit of the election returns in the disputed states. Once completed, individual states would evaluate the Commission's findings and could convene a special legislative session to certify a change in their vote, if needed.[24]

There were tens of thousands of Trump supporters gathered in Washington that day and emotions were running high. One of the biggest beefs was there weren't any courts addressing improprieties.

Two cases were particularly galling. In Wisconsin, the Election Commission sent out instructions that blatantly violated state law to officials statewide about handling mail in ballots. They told clerks they could "fix" mail in ballots that were missing required address data by looking the information up on the internet and writing it in themselves. State law required the ballots to be returned to the voters for any fixes.

The Wisconsin Supreme Court ruled 4-3 that because this had been done in previous elections the Trump campaign could not challenge it. A similar outcome happened in Pennsylvania when the law removing many restrictions on mail in ballots was passed and never validated in accordance with the Pennsylvania Constitution. That state Supreme Court also ruled that the law wasn't challenged in a timely fashion and therefore the violation could not be addressed.

The U.S. Supreme Court refused to even take any challenges by the Trump campaign at all. This infuriated many who saw the actions at state level being dismissed on technicalities as an issue the Supreme Court should deal with. Especially since it could potentially swing the results of the election.

There was also a continued furor over claims that the voting machines had changed results to favor Joe Biden. This remains one of the most contentious issues. It would provide more than the number of votes to change the election results if proven.

All of these factors and a variety of other concerns had the gathered crowds at a fever pitch.

The President addressed the crowd and gave a fiery speech exhorting both his Vice President and Congress to refuse to accept the Electoral College votes. He also told his supporters to follow up this speech with the planned march from the Washington Monument to the Capitol saying:

> I know that everyone will soon be marching over to the Capitol building to peacefully and patriotically make your voices heard...We are going to walk down to the Capitol, and we are going to cheer on our brave senators and congressmen and women, and we are probably not going to be cheering so much for some of them — because you will never take back our country with weakness.[25]

Some Republicans, including Representative Liz Cheney (R-WY), claimed his words incited the crowd:

> The president incited the mob. The president addressed the mob. He lit the flame.[26]

This certainly played a part, but the crowd had come to town disgusted and angry at the lack of attention to legitimate concerns about the election results. When they got to the Capitol, it wasn't long before they tried to enter the building itself. Congress was holding the session to open and count the Electoral College results at that time. The protesters broke windows, pushed through barricades, and quickly overcame the Capitol Police presence.

They entered the Capitol in large numbers and began attempting to enter the chambers where Congress was meeting. That led to an evacuation of the Members and eventually the protesters entered the chambers. Some even posed for photos at the Speaker's dais. They did some minor damage to furniture but overall none of the historic paintings or other artifacts in the building were damaged.

The biggest tragedies were the shooting death of Ashli Babbit, an Air Force veteran who was killed during the chaos, and the subsequent death of Capitol Police officer Brian Sicknick who died from injuries sustained during the assault. Ashli Babbit was unarmed and an investigation is underway to determine if the shooting was justified. The death of Officer Sicknick is likewise under investigation. There were three other deaths among the protesters that day from personal medical conditions not related to violence.

After several hours, the building was cleared with the help of National Guard units. The crowd mostly dispersed in advance of the 6 p.m. curfew imposed by D.C. Mayor Muriel Bowser.

CNN led the media in immediately ramping up the rhetoric:

> CNN officially characterizing today's violence on Capitol Hill today as domestic terrorism.[27]

Other media outlets referred to it as an insurrection. The fact that the label domestic terrorism was used immediately was in stark contrast to their characterizations of the violence and destruction levied on our country by Black Lives Matter and Antifa in 2020. The media never referred to any of that as an insurrection even as federal buildings were attacked repeatedly. They also never classified the assassination of Trump supporter Aaron Danielson by an Antifa member in a planned assault as domestic terrorism.

There was even the comical event when a CNN reporter stood in front of a burning city block in Kenosha, WI, during a BLM/Antifa riot and the graphic read "Fiery but mostly peaceful protests."[28] MSNBC's Ali Velshi also claimed while fires burned behind him in Minneapolis, MN:

> This is mostly a protest. It is not, generally speaking, unruly.[29]

Business owners whose inventories were vandalized and stolen and people who were physically injured beg to differ.

The media shows their clear and dangerous bias in all reporting. The stark difference in immediately escalating their mischaracterizations of the actions people on the Right is a constant problem.

Of note, the Capitol riot was a direct action taken during a Constitutionally mandated function of Congress. It was wrong and it's fair to condemn it accordingly. But when hundreds of Leftist protestors stormed the Senate building during the Constitutional function of Justice Kavanaugh's confirmation hearings in 2018, the media and the entirety of the Left showed no condemnation of the liberal activists.

The Storming of the Capitol, as this is destined to be known, will become an iconic emblem of the end of President Trump's term. It showed that the level of trust in our institutions, the media, the political system, and our ability to conduct fair elections has greatly eroded for many people of the political Right.

That is in many ways justified and will not be easily changed. The question becomes, is this the next stage of an actual insurrection or potential civil war? The odds we will make it to the midterm elections in 2022 without violence are very small. The political options no longer feel sufficient for many to contain the escalating rage.

We need to change that or we could see the violence spiral out of control.

Republicans did amazingly well in the 2020 election, picking up 10 seats in Congress. The truly sad thing is this major win for Conservatives has been almost completely overshadowed by the Biden vs. Trump dispute. We did exceptionally well among Black and Latino voters. That bodes well for our chances to take control of the House of Representatives in the midterms. The safety of the Republic is not only far from lost, it's actually well within our grasp.

It will take new leadership for the Republican party.

The same old establishment running the party organs has proven woefully inadequate to the task of fighting the Democrat slide to

Socialism. We must replace the spineless and corrupt country club consultants who run the party and put some warriors for the American way in their places.

We must organize and register voters, just like the Left has so effectively done. It is vital to show productive Americans that their party is the party of work, responsibility and reward — a new Republican party.

4

THE COMBATANTS

THE BLM/ANTIFA RIOTS OF 2020 and the Storming of the Capitol both show that insurrection is already happening. What constitutes a protest, a riot, an insurrection, a revolution and yes, a Second Civil War?

There are many groups on the Left and Right that qualify as something more than peaceful protesters. Mostly, they tend to be decentralized and lack what could be classified as organization infrastructure. Sometimes this is just an ideological affiliation or even as little as a set of shared grievances or enemies. These groups have been more and more active over the past four years and the violence is escalating.

There has been an active insurrection in Portland, OR against local, state and federal government for more than a year by Antifa. That level of sustained activity is what we must seek to stop and avoid letting any other groups attain that level of velocity. The Storming of the Capitol in January 2021 by supporters of President Trump has been called an insurrection, a coup attempt, and even Domestic Terrorism.

Let's introduce the groups that have been most active on both sides.

THE LEFT

The modern Left is dominated by the Social Justice crowd. Mirroring President Obama, their goal is to tear down and fundamentally transform America.

Every generation wants to feel like they're making the world a better place. The civil rights movement of the 1960s accomplished so much they cast a massive shadow for the new generation. They took on powerful, systematized oppression in this country, and won. In the process they were beaten, attacked by dogs, and even lynched. It was a noble and righteous cause, but there is no institutionalized foe remotely close to that in modern times. Somehow "micro-aggressions" and "mansplaining" don't evoke the same warrior mythos.

This leads to what some call "Selma Envy,"[30] a desire to have a world-beating cause and take on "the man" on behalf of the downtrodden. If that cause doesn't exist, then it must be created. The Left has built a grievance industry that can find or create oppression anywhere. It incubated in academia and slowly spread throughout our educational system. Our schools used to teach life skills like reading, writing and arithmetic that help children succeed as adults. Now they're indoctrination camps where the kids are taught the politically correct ways to think about everything.

The Left is incapable of moderating its tone in response to the progress we have made. Especially since in many ways progressive ideology substitutes for religion inside their liberal bubble. It has a dogma and canon. It must be accepted without reservation and actively practiced or a person risks being shunned as a heretic. Their zeal and fervor in seeking out and burning dissidents is fanatical and resembles the enforcers for a number of totalitarian regimes. In the past, it was taboo for the Left to admit state control and even socialism was their goal. That's no longer the case. The ban has been lifted, especially among the younger crop of activist leaders.

They have been highly successful infusing much of the country with their belief system, but are in some ways victims of that success. They have been emboldened to believe they can push their entire agenda, which includes far too many elements that are anathema to Normal Americans and often counter-Constitutional. Their insularity and confirmation bias have made them immune to seeing the absurdity of many of their efforts and in some ways the SJW movement as a whole.

BLACK LIVES MATTER

The activism powerhouse right now is Black Lives Matter. They rode the wave of the 2020 riots to a massively powerful role in shaping policy on the Left. They are pulling policy far to the radical Left and if you get crosswise with them you'll quickly have a mob calling for your head.

BLM has become such a message that it's hard to determine what it actually is. There is a core BLM organization founded by two avowed Marxists named Patrisse Cullors and Alicia Garza. Their website had provocative statements such as:

> We dismantle the patriarchal practice that requires mothers to work "double shifts" so that they can mother in private even as they participate in public justice work…We disrupt the Western-prescribed nuclear family structure requirement.

They removed these core tenets of their BLM ideology from their website in Summer of 2020.[31] When people interested in the BLM cause researched the organization, many were appalled by what they found. In response, Cullors and Garza didn't change their Marxist views or reevaluate their position on the value of the nuclear family. They deleted it from the website, ensuring their Marxist core remains hidden. They didn't change; they just made sure people can't see what they actually stand for.

The original group is definitely in the revolutionary camp of the BLM world. Even though they started the name, it soon turned into a franchise-style operation and anyone willing to fight for the cause could start a chant and take up the flag. Some of the biggest converts have been the usual suspects of the Lefty world: overeducated white liberals, progressives and now socialists.

It's common now for White people to far outnumber Black people at "BLM" events. Since it's an amorphous, decentralized organism there is no mechanism to sort out who is legit. This leads to some comical situations like rich White kids screaming obscenities in the faces of working class Black cops. If you ever wanted to see the definition of restraint it has to be when those cops don't just club the hippies senseless.

The grievance mongers on the Left are simultaneously telling all these different groups that their beefs matter and they deserve to have them redressed. But then the not-really-homogenous nature of many of these groups comes into play along with competing goals and a limited amount of spoils or attention that any one group can have. So they end up having to endorse Defund the Police and trying to explain how the increase in crime is not a result of that.

Most Americans say they support Black Lives Matter and it seems like such a common-sense thing to do since they are trying to stop the police from slaughtering vast numbers of unarmed innocent Blacks. But, digging a little deeper, it's painfully obvious there is not an epidemic of police killings of unarmed Black people. It just isn't true. This truth corrodes the moral authority they claim.

ANTIFA

Antifa is short for anti-fascist but their goals are much broader than that. In reality, they exist to break things, in this case the entire system of western civilization. The name is derived from Antifaschistische Aktion, a group of Communists in 1930s Weimar Germany. They formed to oppose basically everyone to their political right which included not just the Nazis but also the governing Social Democrats.

The current version of Antifa in the United States is not even that coherent and in many ways lacks logical organization. They have adopted an absurdly broad description of fascist to mean anyone they disagree with including everyone to the right of Marx or Mao.

Antifa has a large number of anarchists and anti-state activists in their midst. This leads to very diffuse organizing and messaging. They try to keep as low a public profile as possible. They communicate on message boards and secure apps to set up their "actions." It's rare for them to have a physical location or meet regularly.

The Rose City Antifa group in Portland, OR, is the oldest known chapter having been around since 2007. They thrive in Portland's extremely liberal environment. Their sustained assaults against federal and city buildings and other emblems of the state were a major feature of the nationwide 2020 riots. Andy Ngo, a journalist at *Post Millennial*, specializes in writing about Antifa. Project Veritas actually infiltrated one of their training sessions for new recruits. This report details some of their tactics.

> How violent is antifa or Rose City Antifa in particular? They do not hesitate to either push back or incite some kind of violence, said the insider. In our classes and in our meetings, before we do any sort of demonstration of black bloc, we talk about weapons detail and what we carry and what we should have.[32]

The lack of an identifiable organization doesn't stop them from being involved in most of the major uprisings in the country. They are usually at the core of any violence that erupts. They travel to them then absorb the local fellow travelers into what becomes a Black Bloc at protests. This is the group dressed in black with helmets, goggles, umbrellas and other makeshift rioting gear like sticks and pipes.

This mob within the mob is usually made up of many different types people from a wide array of backgrounds and ethnicity. The overarching anarchistic nature of Antifa makes a legitimate taxonomy identifying who's who a waste of time. Suffice it to say they are the angriest bunch at any Leftist protest. They are usually the ones who instigate violence by breaking windows and starting the general mayhem. The younger and more militant members from Black Lives Matter often end up in this group as well.

The Antifa Black Bloc presence at protests is a seed for escalation. When large groups of people gather for a common cause, emotions start to run high and bad behavior often follows. Antifa knows that inhibitions against violence drop once a few violent acts occur. They often precipitate a larger degree of destruction by breaking the first glass or literally lighting the fire.

NFAC (NOT F**ING AROUND COALITION)

This is a Black Nationalist group formed by John Fitzgerald Johnson, a former member of the Virginia National Guard. They demand the U.S. turn over the state of Texas to become a Black homeland or other land be provided for that purpose.

They came into the spotlight in 2020 when they began attending marches and protests. Sometimes numbering in the hundreds, the members dress in black fatigues with military style equipment and weapons. They attended events related to the death of Ahmaud Arbery, a Black man killed in Georgia; conducted a march on the Confederate memorial at Stone Mountain, Georgia; and marched in Louisville, Kentucky, at a protest for Breonna Taylor who was killed by police.

None of those actions resulted in violence although there was a negligent discharge of a weapon by one of the members at the event in Louisville that wounded several people.

NEW BLACK PANTHER PARTY

This Black nationalist and separatist group has been around since 1989. They have been involved in a number of controversies including voter intimidation during the 2008 election in Philadelphia, Pennsylvania, when armed members of the group stationed themselves outside polling places.

A former member of the group, Micah Xavier Johnson, shot and killed five police officers and wounded nine others in Dallas, Texas, in July 2016. The officers were providing security for a Black Lives Matter protest when they were killed.

THE RIGHT

The most common theme among activist groups which compose the bulk of participants on the Right is Patriotism and the Constitution. A relative dislike of government interference edging deep into Libertarianism is a commonality. There is a general feeling that individual liberties are being infringed. Some of these groups profess to be holding the line against the decline of the principles America was founded upon. White Supremacists and neo-Nazis are at the extreme fringe end of the spectrum.

PROUD BOYS

They are the best known of the actively militant groups on the Right. They were founded by Canadian media personality Gavin McInnes who named them after a song from the Disney movie *Aladdin* "Proud of Your Boy." Their agenda is hard to pin down and since they've been banned by YouTube, Twitter and Facebook they do not have much of a publicly-facing presence.

They are often characterized as White Supremacist in some way, but that seems difficult to reconcile with the fact that they have been led by Enrique Tarrios, an Afro-Cuban, since 2019. The group is male-only and sometimes professes the belief that western culture is under assault and being destroyed by the Left.

In the past few years, they have arrayed themselves as opposition to the Antifa violence. There have been a number of direct conflicts between the two groups at protests. The Proud Boys began responding to Leftist protests where Antifa was likely to be found and Antifa does the same for events planned by the Right.

This has led to a number of physical confrontations and several knifings. The potential for these to grow larger and more dangerous is wide open. There is not much common ground and little chance the groups can agree to disagree and peacefully coexist.

BOOGALOO BOIS

This anti-government, anti-police movement has a silly name and were dressing in Hawaiian shirts as identification at one point. But it would be a mistake to laugh them off. They have at least two dead law enforcement officers to their discredit.

Active duty Air Force Staff Sergeant Steven Carillo, who claimed affiliation with the group, shot two federal officers outside a courthouse in Oakland, California. Later, he and his associate Robert Justus shot at and used an improvised explosive device against law enforcement officers in Santa Cruz, killing one of them as well.

Their goals seem to be creating chaos to instigate a Second Civil War they call the Boogaloo. Their rationale and grievances are broad and disconnected. They include overreach by the federal government and elements of White Supremacist and even neo-Nazi beliefs. Some believe their movement will lead to a race war.

MILITIA GROUPS

There are a number of groups on the Right that are organized around the idea of militias. We will discuss the definition and actual meaning of the Well Regulated Militia from the Second Amendment in the next chapter. These militias are a separate thing although many of them focus on the Second Amendment as a principle and the Constitution as a whole.

Some of these groups include the Patriot Front, the Rise Above Movement, Three Percenters, Patriot Prayer, and the Oath Keepers. They are regular features at rallies supporting the right to keep and bear arms and opposing government intrusion into personal liberty.

NEO-NAZIS

The less said about these groups the better. But they do exist and their beliefs are heinous. The biggest advantage we have is the FBI watches them closely and keeps informants on the inside to keep on top of any potential violence they may contemplate.

The AtomWaffen Division, Nationalist Socialist Movement, American Nazi Party, Vanguard America, and the Base are groups in this category.

Q ANON

This is a several-year-long online phenomenon where an anonymous government insider known as Q drops information about various issues. The major one is a claim that a cabal of prominent pedophiles including politicians and celebrities have opposed President Trump and plotted against him. They also pushed a number of election-related theories. There have been many other claims and predictions made by Q, but few if any have materialized.

The phrase "Where We Go One, We Go All," often abbreviated as WWG1WGA, is associated with the group. It grew quite large on social media platforms. The tech companies eventually began a campaign to remove the Q followers from their sites.

5

THE ARMED AND WELL

REGULATED MILITIA

WE ARE A LONG WAY from the Right and Left becoming the North and South, but not far enough for anyone to feel safe or comfortable. Major conflicts can grow out of minor skirmishes, especially when there is open violence in the streets. Dozens of killings related to the political unrest have already happened and they are becoming more common. Law and order broke down in several major U.S. cities in 2020. There is no reason to believe the people conducting that violence are going to be appeased by normal legal or political means.

The possibility of extra-political conflict was certainly something our Founders considered and planned for. They integrated the means to stop any enemy, foreign or domestic, in the Constitution even if that enemy is the government itself.

This is **absolutely not** a call for violence of any kind. Actually, it's the exact opposite. It's an attempt to avoid letting the current violence spiral out of control. There are a lot of people bandying about terms like insurrection and domestic terrorism. But what are the definitions, rules, and consequences that accompany any of these actions?

Is it protest, rioting, terrorism, insurgency or insurrection? There are elements of all of those going on in our country right now. We will explore the continuum from peaceful protest to outright armed revolutionary conflict.

Full disclosure, I am a man of the Right and believe in this country's founding principle of protecting individual liberty from state power. I believe America is worth fighting for. I do not believe violence is an acceptable solution to our current differences.

I served in the U.S. Army Special Forces in more than a dozen countries. Both starting and stopping efforts to overthrow governments are part of the U.S .Army Special Forces mission and I have expertise in both.

The cornerstone of Special Forces operations, unconventional warfare is activities conducted to enable a resistance movement or insurgency to coerce, disrupt, or overthrow a government or occupying power…

Special Forces Soldiers are often deployed to prevent terrorist and insurgent incidents abroad. They respond to terrorist activities and train other nations' militaries in the basics of fighting insurgents.[33]

These missions are not conducted here in the United States but the fundamental principles still apply to our current situation. We have groups using violence to further their political causes. We must identify what they are doing and figure out how to stop it.

We need to get a handle on this by isolating the extremists using judicious application of lawful police and security powers. We also need to address the grievances they raise through political and cultural means—sometimes by accepting their concerns and identifying solutions, sometimes by exposing them and their claims as illegitimate. We must facilitate a return to peaceable assembly and petitioning the government for redress of grievances, not destroying things and even killing people to make a point.

The goal here is not to try and bring about some utopian Shangri-La where Left and Right can set aside our differences and frolic together in the fields. We fundamentally disagree on how to live and be governed, so that ain't happening. But in the short term, we need to negotiate some understandings to defuse the volatile times in which we find ourselves. This does not mean we on the Right abandon our principles or the policies we need to implement in order to stop America from being fundamentally transformed.

We can win this fight the right way—in the marketplace of ideas, and at the ballot box. We can regain control of our culture from those on the Left who do not value the America we live in. There are also groups on the Right who believe government has overstepped its bounds and infringes on fundamental liberties. We must band together and stop them both from taking things too far.

If the Right is to prevail, we must fundamentally improve the communication and implementation of the principles we believe in. We must expand our recruitment into groups receptive to the ideas of responsibility, merit-based achievement, rewards based on success, and freedom to live as one wishes as long as that doesn't include hurting others. Winning the hearts and minds of the general populace is key to both ending insurrections and avoiding a civil war.

Not an easy set of tasks, but the alternatives are submission or bloodshed. Clearly, it's worth all the effort we can muster to win this peaceably. I hope we can all agree on that.

THE RULES OF THE GAME

The likelihood of open and extended armed conflict between Americans here on American soil is still extremely low. But the flash point is the highest it has been in a long time. Understanding the legal and historical precedents for the use of force in opposition to government is essential as we plan to tamp down the flames.

The Founders specifically anticipated the possibility citizens might need to rise up and overthrow a government that had become tyrannical.

This was patently obvious to them as they had literally just done so. They realized this required an armed citizenry and ironclad protections stopping the government from disarming them.

The Second Amendment is often considered the most important because it is the only one that provides concrete support for all the others. Without it, the rest of the Bill of Rights is just lofty words on a dusty old parchment nobody reads any more.

At some point, words and rhetoric are no longer the proper tool. Guns are. In the same way the Sons of Liberty took on the greatest military of the 18th century, the British Army and Navy, the free citizens of America must retain the last resort of armed resistance to tyranny.

There is no question this was the Founders' intent, they discussed it often. Without the right to keep and bear arms, they never would have had the opportunity to throw off the yoke of British oppression. They grasped its importance and made damn sure future generations would have the same chance. They ensured no one would be stuck surrendering their weapons and freedom. No midnight knock at the door with government agents there to confiscate their liberty.

There is no mention of target shooting, deer hunting, or any other hobby or sport purpose for this right to be armed. It was 100% related to self-defense, participation in defense of the country as part of the militia. But the most important reason was throwing off any attempt by any government, including our own, to take away the liberties we were all granted by God.

They did not manage to do so in the most easily understandable fashion. Consequently, the very words of the Second Amendment have been a bone of contention for centuries.

A well regulated Militia, being necessary to the security of a free State, the right of the people to keep and bear Arms, shall not be infringed.[34]

Only 27 words to secure Life and Liberty for ourselves and our posterity. That clunky opening clause about a well regulated militia has often been abused and misused by opponents of the Second Amendment. They say this right only applies to service in a government sanctioned militia. This claim completely contradicts the many discussions by the authors about an armed citizenry being necessary to deter or destroy a tyrannical government if one reared its ugly head.

There are two aspects that make the Second Amendment vital to our liberty and pertinent to these discussions. First, it is an individual right granted to each citizen for all purposes other than explicitly illegal activity. Second, it provides the justification for owning weapons that are useful for service in The Militia. This means specifically the private ownership of some weapons of war.

The term "The Militia" used here should be differentiated from the many groups in this country that have adopted the mantle of militia. The well regulated militia in the Second Amendment refers to the collection of all able-bodied citizens available to be called into service to secure the country if circumstances require it.

Groups banded together in support of a political or cultural cause do not become The Militia by adding that name. Even if their cause is to support the Second Amendment and their right to keep and bear arms. The well regulated militia is not a political entity. The numerous private "militia" groups should be thought of as citizens joining in peaceably assembly to petition their government for redress of grievances under the First Amendment.

There is one exception where the "militia" groups and The Militia intersect and it is the most extreme possible: When The Militia organizes itself for the express purpose of overthrowing a government it believes has become tyrannical. This is the most profound act contemplated by the Founders, but there should be no doubt that it was specifically contemplated and the Second Amendment exists to ensure it was at least a possibility.

Fortunately, the late Supreme Court Justice Antonin Scalia provided a bullet-proof defense of the entire Second Amendment from the grammatical attacks and gun grabbing policy makers.

THE INDIVIDUAL RIGHT AND THE MILITIA

Justice Scalia performed many great services to this country in his long and distinguished legal career. None loom larger than his brilliant defense of the Second Amendment in District of Columbia v. Heller.[35] The case was straightforward. DC laws and regulations made it virtually impossible for private citizens to own guns in the District. Richard Heller, a retired cop, filed suit challenging that which was decided in his, and our, favor by the Supreme Court in 2008.

Justice Scalia wrote the majority opinion and it is one of the most powerful pieces of legal writing ever done. He not only obliterated the DC prohibitions, he did the same to every major objection and argument raised by anti-gun activists and the gun-grabbing Left. This opinion provided the legal and historical framework to render them harmless. Although it is not easy reading, it is digestible. At some point, it would be valuable to read through it yourself even if just to admire the work and brilliant reasoning that went into crafting it.

The most important part of the ruling was a rock-solid rationale for the right to keep and bear arms as an individual right, not a collective right for state militias. That had been argued for almost 70 years based on the decision in U.S. v. Miller in 1939.

> Writing for the unanimous Court, Justice James Clark McReynolds reasoned that because possessing a sawed-off double barrel shotgun does not have a reasonable relationship to the preservation or efficiency of a well-regulated militia, the Second Amendment does not protect the possession of such an instrument.[36]

This was used from then on in many cases to claim this allowed the government to regulate virtually any type of weapon. Opponents of the Amendment argued that because the weapon must bear some relation to its use in a state militia, the Second Amendment was, therefore, not an individual right. It was dependent on some connection to a well-regulated, i.e. state-sanctioned, militia.

This was wrong and not in line with either the intentions of the drafters of the Amendment or understanding of most of the terms in use. When Justice Scalia began to set out his case, he dug all the way back to English Common Law and the writings of the Founders and members of Congress involved in drafting the document. He researched the origins and common meanings of words like militia, arms, and well-regulated. He did the homework and found an unmistakable intent and granting to we, the people, of an individual right to keep and bear arms.

> The Second Amendment protects an individual right to possess a firearm unconnected with service in a militia, and to use that arm for traditionally lawful purposes, such as self-defense within the home.[37]

Thank you, Justice Scalia! This reversed 70 years of misinterpretation since U.S. v. Miller and removed one of the main attacks by the gun grabbers. It was an individual right.

The text of the Second Amendment had left this avenue of attack open due to the obscure nature of its construction and the lack of understanding what militia, arms, and well-regulated meant to its drafters.

> A well regulated Militia, being necessary to the security of a free State….

The presence of well regulated and militia in the prefatory clause led many to argue this called explicitly for this right to be subordinate to state control of militias. Justice Scalia immediately put that mistaken conclusion to rest.

> The militia comprised all males physically capable of acting in concert for the common defense. The Antifederalists feared that the Federal Government would disarm the people in order to disable this citizens' militia, enabling a politicized standing army or a select militia to rule. The response was to deny Congress power to abridge the ancient right of individuals to keep and bear arms, so that the ideal of a citizens' militia would be preserved.

That powerful paragraph made certain no subsequent government could remove a citizen's right to keep and bear arms.

The back and forth about why well-regulated is included in the text has often come up in attempts to justify some gun control measure or another. Justice Scalia again showed that when the Amendment was written, well-regulated meant the same as well-trained. It actually meant the weapons needed to be owned and used regularly by the individuals who become the militia in time of danger. This guarantees they didn't need to rely on permission from any level of government to own and operate their guns.

The wins just keep piling up here for people who believe the Constitution means what it says. But we aren't done, not by a long shot (pun intended).

Another big argument has been what weapons the government can legally ban since muskets were the most common firearm in existence at the time. Obviously, some level of restriction on private ownership seems wise unless we are fine with a neighbor owning an Apache gunship or a nuclear weapon. I'm fine with me owning these things, the rest of you, not so much. Joking, just joking. Therefore we must establish where the line is and how do we maintain it as technology changes?

This was another major coup by Justice Scalia as there was sufficient historical precedent and intent shown by the drafters. He correctly decided the proper standard was a weapon in common use and suitable for service as a member of the militia when needed. The ruling states:

Miller's holding that the sorts of weapons protected are those in common use at the time finds support in the historical tradition of prohibiting the carrying of dangerous and unusual weapons.

Dangerous and unusual includes your neighbor's fully-armed Apache gunship (not mine) and nuclear weapon as well as a number of other lesser but still unusual guns like those covered in the National Firearms Act of 1934.

Firearms subject to the 1934 Act included shotguns and rifles having barrels less than 18 inches in length, certain firearms described as any other weapons, machine guns, and firearm mufflers and silencers.[38]

There was never a lot of serious argument about individuals having the right to own tanks or fighter jets. That mostly came up when those arguing to ban more weapons would disingenuously claim that if we can't ban an AR-15 then citizens could own whatever weapons they want. Obviously not true, but it did show a need for a standard that could be both universal and timeless. Justice Scalia offered clarification with the phrase "in common use at the time."

He didn't invent the concept, but he put it in context showing that for a militia to be effective i.e. well-regulated, the members had to show up with weapons useful to their role as individual soldiers. That was a musket of some sort when the amendment was drafted. Times change and so did the personal weapon of the individual soldier as well as the weapons in common use at the time. Right there is your timeless standard.

Today the individual soldier carries some type of AR-15 style rifle with a large capacity, detachable box magazine. It just so happens that the most commonly-used weapon by private citizens, also known as the well-regulated militia, is some type of AR-15 style rifle with a large capacity, detachable box magazine. Interesting.

The gun grabbers have hit a wall since D.C. v. Heller because of this magnificent combination of historical reference and legal reasoning. It would be virtually impossible for an Assault Weapons Ban like the one in 1994 to be passed. It banned many military-style features on guns and the sale of large-capacity magazines. But these were part of these weapons' usefulness for service in The Militia.

Even if one could be passed, it has not been shown it would be effective. The results of the previous ban were minimal at best based on a government study of its usefulness.

An Updated Assessment of the Federal Assault Weapons Ban: Impacts on Gun Markets and Gun Violence, 1994-2003 Report to the

National Institute of Justice, United States Department of Justice. This conclusion says it all:

Should it be renewed, the ban's effects on gun violence are likely to be small at best and perhaps too small for reliable measurement.[39]

Another area of contention with dissenting justices was about the meaning of "keep and bear arms." There was an attempt by the losing side in their dissent to claim "bear arms" meant serve in a military unit, hence a collective right, not an individual one. Justice Scalia had many other arguments proving it was not the case, but this was an elegant bit of jurisprudentially wicked snark. He used Justice Ginsburg's own words from another ruling to smack them down.

At the time of the founding, as now, to bear meant to carry. ...We think that JUSTICE GINSBURG accurately captured the natural meaning of bear arms. Although the phrase implies that the carrying of the weapon is for the purpose of offensive or defensive action, it in no way connotes participation in a structured military organization.

He goes on to eviscerate the rest of their attempt to evade the clear meaning of bear arms. It obviously means to carry them about, and he points this out with some more entertaining, intra-justice banter.

In any event, the meaning of bear arms that petitioners and JUSTICE STEVENS propose is not even the (some times) idiomatic meaning. Rather, they manufacture a hybrid definition, whereby bear arms connotes the actual carrying of arms (and therefore is not really an idiom) but only in the service of an organized militia. No dictionary has ever adopted that definition, and we have been apprised of no source that indicates that it carried that meaning at the time of the founding. But it is easy to see why petitioners and the dissent are driven to the hybrid definition. Giving bear Arms its idiomatic meaning would cause the protected right to consist of the right to be a soldier or to wage war—an absurdity that no commentator has ever endorsed. [40]

It was a weak attempt to hamstring the right and one Justice Scalia dispensed with strongly and completely. There would be no infringing on the keeping or bearing of arms.

The reason for the Second Amendment and its history is also detailed. One specific and important detail being that it was not a new right.

Meaning of the Operative Clause.

Putting all of these textual elements together, we find that they guarantee the individual right to possess and carry weapons in case of confrontation. This meaning is strongly confirmed by the historical background of the Second Amendment. We look to this because it has always been widely understood that the Second Amendment, like the First and Fourth Amendments, codified a pre-existing right.[41]

Americans already possessed the right to keep and bear arms. The Second Amendment just made sure it was written down. They knew people would come along looking for ways to increase state power. They wanted to make sure we had a document to roll up and poke them in the eye with.

In pursuing this explanation, Justice Scalia leads us down the path of a tyrannical government seeking to disarm their citizens in order to better control them. As English citizens, the colonists benefitted from a hard-won freedom designed to stop the Crown from oppressing the people by force.

...the Declaration of Right (which was codified as the English Bill of Rights), that Protestants would never be disarmed...This right has long been understood to be the predecessor to our Second Amendment.

The genesis of our Second Amendment was the ability of citizens to protect against an overly-oppressive central government. The colonists were well aware of what could happen to them.

Between the Restoration and the Glorious Revolution, the Stuart Kings Charles II and James II succeeded in using select militias loyal to them to suppress political dissidents, in part by disarming their opponents.

That was why the Founders were dead set against giving any power to the state that would allow it to be the sole purveyor of force. They made sure to put a positive restriction against infringing the people's right to be armed.

> During the 1788 ratification debates, the fear that the federal government would disarm the people in order to impose rule through a standing army or select militia was pervasive in Antifederalist rhetoric… It was understood across the political spectrum that the right helped to secure the ideal of a citizen militia, which might be necessary to oppose an oppressive military force if the constitutional order broke down.

The number one reason for all of this was:

> [W]hen the able-bodied men of a nation are trained in arms and organized, they are better able to resist tyranny.[42]

This hasn't needed to be tested yet, but that was clearly the intent of the Founders and drafters of the Bill of Rights. They knew that once again in the course of human events it might became necessary for one people to dissolve the political bands that connect them to another. The only real way that option exists is with an armed citizenry.

THE MILITIA IN EXTREMIS

It is always interesting to argue with gun grabbers about just how an armed revolt in America might work. Their initial bloviation is usually along the lines of "How's that AR-15 gonna do against a tank, loser?" Not very well in a direct fire engagement, but that is not how this would likely play out.

Imagine a scenario where citizens are oppressed to the point they consider redressing their grievances by removing the oppressors. There would need be some cataclysmic abuse of our Constitutional rights to make this progress beyond the lunatic fringe.

Here are a couple of believable worst-case scenarios. If Hillary Clinton had been sworn in as President in January of 2017, she could have immediately replaced the deceased Justice Antonin Scalia with former Obama Attorney General Eric Holder, Justice Kennedy with another former Obama Attorney General Loretta Lynch, and Justice Ginsburg with a much younger and more progressively activist replacement like Representative Rashida Tlaib (D-MI). The freedoms we enjoy due by the Constitution would cease to exist as we know them.

Or the more recent plan advanced by a number of influential leaders on the Left to "pack the Court" if they control the Presidency and Congress. The general concept is that Congress passes a bill adding more justices and the President signs it. This has not been done since the end of the Civil War when the current number of nine justices was set. President Franklin Delano Roosevelt tried to do it in 1937 to override some rulings against his New Deal policies. He was stopped by members of his own party.

When asked if he would pack the court if given the opportunity, Presidential candidate Joe Biden refused to answer during the 2020 campaign. The anger on the Left over the replacement of extremely liberal Justice Ginsburg with extremely conservative Justice Amy Coney Barrett has made this a distinct possibility. Adding four liberal judges to the mix would tip the balance to 7-6 in the Democrats' favor.

Either of those would give a liberal activist majority on the court. It is then possible to envision them immediately working to fix that pesky Second Amendment. D.C. v. Heller be damned, they would be able to rule on a case challenging it and throw it right out the window. Individual rights: Gone. Well-regulated militia: Gone. National Guard only. Keep and Bear Arms: Gone. Only for the military and police. They might leave the Second Amendment on the books, but only so they didn't have to renumber the rest after completely stripping it of all meaning and usefulness in defending liberty.

Next, the Democrat-controlled House and Senate ram through a bill banning all firearms for private use and allowing for confiscation. No grandfather clauses, just turn them all in.

Is this an overly-extreme scenario? Not really. The only variable would be if they decided to let the peasantry keep their muskets for hunting and home defense. Maybe revolvers and bolt-action rifles would make the cut. But the actuality of an armed citizenry capable of challenging a tyrannical government would be effectively over.

Or would it?

If this situation came to pass, an attempt to overthrow that oppressive regime would not be out of the question. I'm not advocating it even in this extreme situation. But that would seem to be the type of tyranny by a central government our Founders had in mind.

Here is why the talk about this fictional Militia going head to head with an F-16 is silly. The Leftists assume the U.S. military would side with this government in this naked power grab. It likely would at an institutional level. But there are many members of the military who would see this as an un-Constitutional and therefore unlawful assault on the very document they swore to protect and defend.

Legally the Constitution would be still intact since the proper procedures for gutting it had been followed. There is a strong case to be made that all military members would still owe their oath to this new, and meaningless, document. I can tell you from discussions with many active duty military, national guard, and veterans, there are plenty who would not accept that emasculated agreement.

There is a large sentiment in agreement with the statement previously that the Second Amendment secures all the rest. If that is removed, then the Constitution itself is no longer the same document they swore to protect and defend. That oath also included "…against all enemies, foreign and domestic."

It is not hard to imagine a collection of new Sons of Liberty rising up to defend the citizens and help dissolve the political bands that once joined us. Or even just running the bums who had desecrated our liberty out of town. If these Constitutional defenders made the call to arms then an answer could come from some members of the military or veterans. Perhaps in the form of seizing a National Guard armory or even an active duty base, for some reason Texas keeps coming to mind.

Once some of the heavy tools of military combat were in the hands of a group supporting the Constitution, the truth could change considerably. It is entirely possible that other military units would refuse to attack them and some might even join them.

Even if the rebellion only turns into a guerrilla effort using hit and run and ambush techniques, it would still leave potentially millions of armed, trained, and effective fighters for what remained of the central government to deal with. That is a highly dangerous situation for a government that has to protect all elements of the infrastructure that runs this massively complex thing we call America.

We have been blessed by large oceans keeping our enemies well away so we have not had to fortify or secure the interior of this country. We are essentially one giant, soft target. It would be an almost insurmountable task for the remnants of the oppressive regime to contain a free range rebellion.

Let me reiterate this is a doomsday scenario. It is irksome when the least militarily-competent people in the country deny the possibility of such a thing. It's not impossible and it's no more of a long shot than a rag tag collection of farmers and merchants armed with their own personal weapons defeating the massive fighting power of the British Empire's Army and Navy at the height of its power.

WELCOME TO THE WELL REGULATED MILITIA

If you're reading this book, there is a decent chance you're already a member of The Militia in good standing. It consists of all able-bodied males 17-45 and those under 65 who have previously served in the Armed Forces. It also includes all women serving in the National Guard. This is written in 10 U.S. Code § 246 - Militia: composition and classes.[43] Clearly, it has not been updated to reflect gender equality which is a major fail in the existing law.

This gender distinction is a relic of the times in which it was written and it is highly doubtful it would stand up to legal challenge. Justice Scalia's ruling was clear on the weapon of the day allowing an AR-15 rather than the musket. In keeping with this intent, the law shouldn't exclude women in the 21st century when the exclusion is based on 18th century standards. The parallel is the AR-15 did not exist then nor did women's rights. Both do now therefore both should have equal Second Amendment inclusion. Age restrictions fall into this same category. Both are due an upgrade to represent equal rights under the law.

This Militia of the United States is not dependent on the government to constitute or control it, it simply exists. Why did the Founders think this was so important? Easy, they wanted to make sure we could overthrow any government that became unreasonably oppressive, period. Everything else is just icing on the weapon of war. Fighting and winning a revolutionary war for freedom left an indelible memory of how and why an armed citizenry would always be necessary.

It's a lot of fun to make that point with coastal Leftists. They truly hate the idea that what they consider the unwashed rabble of flyover country, known to the rest of us as the Midwestern States, could someday rise up and undo any "fundamental transformation" of this country by the Liberal Left. "How dare they?" Oh, we dare and if they somehow manage to cheat the Constitution badly enough they will find out just how daring we are.

To be fair, The Militia shares equal responsibility for securing the country from threats under a Constitutionally sound government, as well. Things like the Canadians getting all hopped up on Molson and Tim Hortons donuts and rolling snowmobiles across the border, or a natural disaster so epic it overwhelmed the capabilities of the police, or say nationwide riots the police were unable or ordered not to control.

But never for a second doubt that the Second Amendment exists to facilitate a potential overthrow of a tyrannical government. That should be a sobering thought for anyone.

6

THE CURRENT

INSURRECTIONS

WHEN DOES PEACEFUL PROTEST and petitioning the government for redress of grievances become insurrection or sedition? Are the violent acts committed in the current conflict domestic terrorism or an internal insurgency? Those are complicated concepts that unfortunately we are watching play out on the streets of this country.

The idea that we are fighting an insurgency in America may seem strange. OK, it is strange. But let's walk through the current situation and see if the description makes sense and is helpful.

It bears a reminder that while we think of the American Revolution as the war that created this country, the Sons of Liberty insurgency predated and led to that conflict. It was an underground movement founded by Samuel Adams in 1765 in response to British taxation. In the intervening eleven years leading up to the Declaration of Independence, it conducted both information operations and sabotage against the British. Many leaders of the American Revolution filtered through its ranks as it gained support.

And most importantly, they won, a fact we can all be thankful for. It also shows that a small but determined band of true believers can overcome incredible odds and prevail. We would be foolish to ignore that possibility and say it could never happen in modern times. It is highly unlikely an armed insurrection will take over America in the near term and our goal here is to avoid one. But there is violent resistance underway on both sides of the political spectrum and neither side is likely to be appeased by normal political means.

The protests and riots that occurred in the past year plus may have risen to the level of insurrection and even domestic terrorism. That includes actions by both Antifa/BLM throughout 2020 as well as the storming of the Capitol in January 2021. Let's look at those and then evaluate how they should be properly classified and what type of response might be most effective.

THE 2020 RIOTS

Violence during the 2020 Riots and after the election escalated to truly dangerous levels. We can use the concepts of insurgency, counterinsurgency, and terrorism to evaluate the threats and plan smart responses moving forward.

THE MOTIVATIONS OF THE LEFT

Elements of the Left, mostly Black Lives Matter and Antifa, protested and rioted on a scale unseen in modern U.S. history. Anger caused by three main issues fueled this:

Perceived police violence

Anti-Trump sentiment

COVID-19 quarantine mania

To some extent there were valid concerns in all three areas, but there was also a huge influx of mis- and dis-information. This helped cause a perfect storm of righteous indignation that motivated massive numbers of people to violently take to the streets.

All of this combined to throw figurative fuel and create literal fires.

GEORGE FLOYD AND POLICE VIOLENCE

The protests, which quickly became riots, began in response to the killing of George Floyd in Minneapolis, MN, by police. This was deemed to be part of an epidemic of police killings of unarmed Black people. That narrative is widely accepted even though it is not borne out by a careful examination of the facts and statistics about police shootings. The main charge levied by Black Lives Matters was that policing in America is infected with systemic racism.

Security Studies Group (SSG) did a study of police killings to determine if that claim was valid. First, SSG determined that the facts did not support the claim of rampant institutional police violence toward Black people. In 2019, 14 unarmed Black people were killed by police nationwide. Fourteen is not an epidemic. Almost all of those involved a person killed while committing an act of violence against the police or a civilian at the time.[44]

Second, using disparate outcome, like saying this happens to Blacks more than their percentage of the population, does not prove anything about its cause. It's essential to look at all the elements that could have led to the statistical difference. SSG did and as it turned out there were at least three factors with higher correlation to more Black people being killed than systemic racism.

Those were:

1. Being male

2. Being in a high crime neighborhood

3. Being in the act of committing a violent crime

This doesn't prove there are not problems in many police forces that need to be dealt with. It also doesn't prove that racism is not a problem in some of them. It does, however, show that the main claim by BLM that unjustified police killings of Black people has reached epidemic proportions is unproven.

The combination of video of the Floyd killing and widespread use of the false epidemic narrative by media and on social media created the frenzy that started the protests. Similar outpourings of anger had occurred after other police killings. Black Lives Matter itself was formed in response to the police killing of Michael Brown in St. Louis, Missouri. This incident and the subsequent riots were largely publicized using the false claim Brown was shot with his hands raised. "Hands up, Don't Shoot" became a rallying cry.

The Floyd protests in Minneapolis grew and turned into riots that spread nationwide.

ANTI-TRUMP SENTIMENT

The political Left and their media collaborators spent four years demonizing President Trump in a truly unprecedented fashion. Whether you supported Trump or not it is difficult to see how press coverage that was more than 90% negative gave an accurate portrayal. Granted, Trump was often his own worst enemy and caused many of his own problems, but there was a truly pathological hatred of the man that was cultivated and spread by the Left.

That played into the furor around the protests. The claim Trump was a racist and part of the larger problem of Systemic Racism dovetailed nicely with the BLM narrative that police violence was just a symptom of a larger national oppression.

The fact we were deep into a massively contentious election season already had tensions at a fever pitch. Floyd's death served as a catalyst and cause celebre for most of the Left to coalesce around.

COVID-19 QUARANTINE MANIA

Nothing like COVID has happened in 100 years and never with the incredible connectivity we all have now through social media. We were all forced into physical isolation but given free rein to converse and complain about it with everyone.

The damage and disruption the virus has caused is difficult to even comprehend. The death toll is stunning, the economic disruption is massive, and the emotional distress is real and poorly handled.

The emotional toll of COVID-19 helped blow a collective gasket for the Left. They took all of their pent-up rage at unresolved grievances and hit the streets.

THE ANTIFA ELEMENT

Antifa was present at almost every place the protests turned into riots. The Black Bloc of their angriest rioters formed the nucleus of most of the violent mobs. They often cross-pollinated with the BLM crowd, attracting the worst elements of it to get a high pitch of frenzy going.

The amount of damage in the 2020 riots went easily into the billions of dollars. It would be challenging to separate out who did more damage between Antifa/Black Lives Matter and looters. The destruction was so widespread and interconnected that many parts of major cities looked literally like war zones. The Antifa/BLM Bloc usually instigated the violence and destruction that led looters to feel safe joining in once the chaos reached a certain level.

Their ongoing insurrection in Portland gave a continuity to the somewhat sporadic violence across the rest of the country. They also seized a chunk of downtown Seattle and named it Capitol Hill Autonomous Zone (CHAZ) then changed the name to Capitol Hill Organized Protest (CHOP). This planting of a flag gave a glimpse into their aspirations. It also showed what happens when law enforcement goes passive. The bad elements advance. Although the media refused to accurately report on the conditions inside the barricade, the reality of violent crimes including murder and rape eventually surfaced.

THE RIGHT

While the 2020 Riots were largely conducted by the Left, there were responses to them from groups on the Right. Many of these same groups have an ongoing beef with the Left but also in many cases with the government. That led to some protests against COVID restrictions, with especially active ones in Michigan, which in some cases involved armed participants and criminal activity.

RESPONSE TO RIOTS

There were multiple instances of right wing groups attending protests and hot spots in the 2020 Riots. The usual rallying cry was to oppose the violence that was being conducted and substitute for little or no police response. This led to confrontations between them and Antifa/BLM.[45]

The bulk were street fights but several times they escalated into bloodshed. Fatal occurrences included the incident in Kenosha where Kyle Rittenhouse killed two Antifa/BLM mob members who attacked him and the killing in Portland of a Patriot Prayer member by Antifa.

There were more killings and an unsettling amount of violence. Somehow none of them turned into open gun battles although that possibility becomes more likely as both sides now tend to be armed.

COVID RESTRICTION PROTESTS

The government-ordered lockdowns and mask requirements indirectly led to numerous protests around the country which were mostly peaceful. One of the larger occurred in Michigan on April 15, 2020. Tax day is an important date for anti-government groups. It was called Operation Gridlock and several thousand people surrounded the state Capitol and jammed the surrounding streets with vehicles.

A follow-on event on April 30th involved armed people in tactical gear entering the state Capitol itself which did not have a restriction against open carry of weapons. While completely legal, the incident gave a decidedly more militant feel to the protests. Many Michigan lawmakers were upset and the media used the pictures of armed, masked

WINNING *the* SECOND CIVIL WAR

protesters in the Capitol to imply they had taken it by force.

Later in the year, the FBI made a number of arrests in a plot to kidnap Michigan Governor Gretchen Whitmer and attack the state government over the restrictions she put in place. The plan was outlandish, but they did conduct preliminary surveillance and planning. They had been infiltrated by an FBI informant and stopped before they conducted any of the intended crimes.

In October 2020, the Michigan Supreme Court ruled that Governor Whitmer had violated the state Constitution with many of the restrictions and ordered her to remove them. This validated the beliefs of many that government had greatly overstepped its bounds.

THE 2021 STORMING OF THE CAPITOL

The Stop the Steal (StS) event on Jan 6, 2021 was organized to consist of speeches protesting the election results at the Washington Monument followed by a march to the Capitol. Hundreds of thousands gathered to hear President Trump and others speak about the topic and then to protest the counting of the Electoral College slates in Congress.

The protest focused on many theories that claim the election was stolen. There was also considerable unhappiness with the lack of any judicial remedies. President Trump propagated many of these theories and called on supporters to refuse to accept them. There were efforts to ensure the fraud and abuses claimed were investigated and the results were overturned. This led to questions regarding whether he incited violence among his supporters. His statement during the speech:

"I know that everyone here will soon be marching over to the Capitol building to peacefully and patriotically make your voices heard."

Seems to make a case for incitement difficult. After the speeches, the crowd moved up to the Capitol and escalated into a riot that ended up with multiple assaults on Capitol Police and other law enforcement including the death of one officer and one of the protesters.

There has been a concerted effort from all members of the Leftist coalition to treat this event as an unprecedented assault on our very

Republic. They seem to forget that in January 2012, several thousand Occupy DC leftist protesters stormed Congress. They trapped numerous members and their staff in their offices. My wife was among those confronted by the mob. She was not intimidated and they failed to "occupy" the office she stood watch over.

CASUALTIES OF THE CURRENT VIOLENCE

There have been a significant number of deadly and otherwise violent incidents since the start of the 2020 riots.

Individual affiliations with the groups involved cannot always be definitively determined. In those cases, apparent associations are presented in the following incidents based on circumstances and context.

THE KYLE RITTENHOUSE CASE

Incident: Joseph Rosenbaum and Anthony Huber were shot and killed by Kyle Rittenhouse in Kenosha, Wisconsin, on August 25, 2020. Gaige Grosskreutz was wounded.

Scenario: The shooting of Jacob Blake, a Black man in Kenosha, sparked protests and riots there. Kyle Rittenhouse, a 17-year-old from Antioch, Illinois, worked in Kenosha and joined a friend from Kenosha in answering a call to protect local businesses from the wrath of violent mobs. The friend provided Rittenhouse with an AR-15 and they joined members of a local group called the "Kenosha Guard" in securing the car dealership.

Rittenhouse was accosted and chased by Joseph Rosenbaum that night. A shot was fired from behind Rittenhouse. Rittenhouse turned and Rosenbaum closed on him attempting to take his weapon. Rittenhouse warned he was going to shoot but to no avail. He fired several shots, killing Rosenbaum. Rittenhouse immediately began providing emergency aid to downed Rosenbaum then called 911 stating what had just occurred.

The other protesters in the area began yelling "get him" and other aggressive statements. Rittenhouse felt he was in danger and started running again. While being chased by multiple protesters, he tripped and fell. Anthony Huber beat him with a skateboard and as Huber regrouped Rittenhouse shot and killed him. Then Gaige Grosskreutz pulled a pistol in close proximity and Rittenhouse shot and wounded him.

Groups involved: Black Lives Matter, Antifa, Kenosha Guard (informal militia).

None of the principal individuals in this incident have official ties to these groups, but the three individuals shot were participating in the Antifa/BLM protest/riots. Rittenhouse was an avid supporter of the police and in the same vicinity of the Kenosha Guard although that organization claims no affiliation with him.

Evaluation: Rittenhouse was charged with First Degree Murder which does not seem justified as there is no evidence he intended to kill anyone. He was a minor in possession of a weapon in apparent violation of Wisconsin law which makes 18 the minimum age. But there are exceptions to that for hunting, target shooting, etc. It's unclear if those will apply to him.

The defense that Rittenhouse was acting in legitimate self-defense will be made and is supported by a number of factors. Rittenhouse was obviously attempting to retreat from Rosenbaum. The shot fired in close proximity behind him would give him a reasonable claim to fear for his life. Rosenbaum was clearly the aggressor and the attempt to take the weapon was an immediate threat.

I have trained civilians, police tactical units, and military hostage rescue units. I would judge this as legitimate self-defense if presented as a shoot/no shoot scenario during training.

Implications: This direct and deadly confrontation between members of the activist Left and Right shows the danger of escalation at protests. It also shows what happens when law enforcement fails to secure Americans and their businesses. The risk of deadly incidents increases significantly when angry, often un-trained, people square off in chaotic situations.

THE MICHAEL REINOEHL CASE

Incident: Aaron "Jay" Danielson, a Pro-Trump protester, was shot and killed by Antifa member Michael Forest Reinoehl in Portland, Oregon, on August 29, 2020.

Scenario: Riots by Antifa/BLM and related anarchists had been ongoing in downtown Portland for months. The right-wing group Patriot Prayer organized a vehicle caravan as a counter-protest and to support President Trump. The caravan organizers initially planned to stay out of the downtown Portland area but eventually the group headed downtown.

The caravan was attacked by Antifa/BLM supporters who threw objects at the vehicles from highway overpasses and from the side of the road. The caravan members shot paintballs and sprayed pepper spray at the Antifa/BLM personnel.

Later that evening, Danielson and another member of Patriot Prayer were walking in downtown Portland when they were approached by Reinoehl who shot and killed Danielson and then fled the scene.

Reinoehl was killed on September 3, 2020, by law enforcement serving an arrest warrant. He was armed and attempted to evade capture.

Reinoehl was interviewed by Vice magazine between these two events. In the video, he clearly admitted murdering Danielson. He said, "I see a civil war right around the corner. That shot felt like the beginning of a war."

Groups involved: Antifa, Patriot Prayer.

Reinoehl was a well-known member of the Antifa mob that had been conducting regular riots. He wrote in a June 2020 Instagram post that he was "100% ANTIFA all the way!" He also had a Black Power fist neck tattoo, even though he was White, but there was no evidence that he associated with BLM. He denied Antifa affiliation in the Vice interview, claiming that he wasn't a joiner. But he was as much a member of Antifa as anyone is in that largely anarchistic organization.

Danielson was a member of Patriot Prayer and wearing a ball cap with their logo when he was murdered. He was from a racially-mixed neighborhood and his many Black acquaintances from that neighborhood denied he had any White Supremacist tendencies.

Evaluation: From the publicly-available information this appears to have been a straight-up execution. There is security camera footage showing Reinoehl stalking Danielson and Reinoehl made no mention of any provocation in his Vice interview.

Reinoehl had a history of run-ins with law enforcement. He had been arrested twice for weapon possession and once while speeding at over 100 mph with children and drugs in the car. He was an unstable, serial criminal who was involved in some of the most violent aspects of the ongoing Portland Riots.

The Patriot Prayer group has had an ongoing feud with Antifa for years. The caravan was largely a response borne out of disgust that the police were not stopping the Antifa riots in Portland. The two groups had clashed numerous times previously when one would crash the other's event.

The fact that Reinoehl will not be tried for the murder is unfortunate. The legal process would have given some insight into the inner workings of both groups during discovery and a trial.

Implications: Portland is ground zero as the most likely place for a full-scale violent battle. It has the largest number of free-range Antifa and associates and it has been at the forefront of news coverage regarding its ongoing lawlessness.

To the Left, it represents the power of their movement to paralyze law enforcement and civic authorities. The police were held at bay in a purely defensive posture for months and even the arrival of federal forces to help protect the justice buildings did not stop the riots. They may not have won any actual battles but Antifa's anarchy wing won major symbolic strength. They continued their attacks, maintained their stronghold, and were not pushed out.

To the Right, Portland represents the same thing, but in a very negative way. The more extreme right-wing militia groups actually share a disdain for the federal government. But when the forces of the socialist

Left attack them, the enemy of my enemy becomes my friend. The Patriot Prayer group and others like it see Portland as enemy-occupied territory and the urge to counterattack and set it free is growing.

THE DANIEL PERRY CASE

Incident: Garrett Foster was shot and killed by active duty U.S. Army Sergeant Daniel Perry in Austin, Texas, on July 25, 2020.

Scenario: Garrett Foster was participating in a BLM march in Austin. He is White and was pushing his Black girlfriend in a wheelchair. He was armed with an AK-47 variant rifle.

Daniel Perry was working as an Uber driver during his off-duty time to earn extra money that night.

Perry came up to an intersection that was blocked by the Black Lives Matter protesters. As he attempted to turn a corner they swarmed his car and began beating it. Foster was in that group and aimed his rifle at Perry who then shot him.

Groups involved: Black Lives Matter, individual person

Foster qualifies as a BLM member under the rules we are applying to these groups. He and his girlfriend were well known to BLM and often participated in activities supporting the group.

Perry was a member of the U.S. Army but that was not known to any of those who swarmed the vehicle. He was in Austin for personal commercial reasons and so that affiliation is not relevant except to the extent it prepared him to defend himself.

Evaluation: The mobbing of cars by protesters and the blocking of thoroughfares was a regular occurrence in 2020. By the time this incident happened, multiple motorists had been attacked and one was even shot in his vehicle while surrounded by a mob in Provo, Utah.

It is unknown whether Perry was aware of that particular incident, but he was obviously aware of the imminent danger when the mob surrounded his vehicle. He knew he faced an immediate deadly threat when Foster raised the rifle and aimed at him. Both of those factors satisfy the requirement for a ruling that shooting Foster was an act of self-defense.

The protesters claimed that Perry tried to ram his way through the crowd and was speeding. The available footage does not support those allegations, although he was attempting to move through the crowd to turn.

Implications: Blocking streets and highways has become a common tactic by protesters who consider it civil disobedience. In actuality it's an escalation point toward a riot as it illegally impedes travel and could also be classified as domestic terrorism. Vehicle destruction and violent assaults on drivers trapped by the crowd have been happening far too regularly.

This has led to increased incidents of drivers moving through these crowds in pursuit of personal safety even if it means hitting the protesters with the vehicle. Given the precedent of violent attacks that have occurred, a determination of self-defense due to legitimate fear of great bodily harm should apply.

In this case, Foster's semi-automatic rifle made that claim much easier to defend. But the level of tolerance by non-protesters for crowds blocking streets and worse, enveloping motorists with a mob, is dropping rapidly.

The real and very frightening danger of being trapped and then attacked is likely to create more incidents where motorists use the law of tonnage to escape the mob.

THE STEPHAN CANNON CASE

Incident: David Dorn, a retired St. Louis, Missouri, Police Captain, was shot and killed by Stephan Cannon on August 27, 2020.

Scenario: Retired Captain Dorn provided private security for the owner of a pawn shop who was a former criminal Dorn had personally helped get on the right path when he was still a serving officer. Dorn responded to an alarm at the pawn shop and came upon a group of looters including Cannon who shot him and left him to die on the street.

Groups involved: Criminals, individual person.

Evaluation: There is no indication the killers knew Dorn was a retired St. Louis police officer. They were engaged in criminal activity as opposed to organized protests. Although this may seem unrelated, the general aura of lawlessness, chaos, and impunity pervasive throughout the country caused by the riots has opened the floodgate for other criminals. This was organized looting that exploited an existing politically-motivated event.

Implications: Criminals have ample opportunity to exploit situations like this with a decent chance they will get away with it. This incident highlights the necessity for effective law enforcement.

THE STEVEN CARRILLO CASE

Incidents: Deval Patrick Underwood and Sheriff Sergeant Damon Gutzwiller were shot and killed on May 29, 2020 in Oakland, California and on June 6, 2020 in Santa Cruz, California, respectively.

Scenario: Steven Carrillo, an active duty Air Force sergeant, and Robert Justus conducted a drive by shooting at the Oakland Federal Courthouse, killing Underwood and wounding the other officer on duty with him. Police went to Carrillo's residence a week later to arrest him, where he shot and killed Gutzwiller and wounded another officer. Carrillo attempted to escape by vehicle. He got into a shootout with California Highway Patrol officers, deploying a pipe bomb that wounded one of them.

Carrillo scrawled Boogaloo-related messages on his vehicle in his own blood after being wounded.

Groups involved: Boogaloo, law enforcement.

Evaluation: The officers at the Oakland Courthouse were both uniformed security officers on contract with Federal Protective Services. Carrillo had ties to the Boogaloo movement on social media and among items police found at his home. This appears to be direct targeting of federal officers for a cause. Department of Homeland Security Deputy Secretary Ken Cucinelli accurately called the attack domestic terrorism.

Implications: There are many targets for a motivated killer in the United States. We can't protect them all. We need to focus on interdicting the extremists before they act and delivering swift verdicts and appropriate punishment when they do.

THE STORMING THE CAPITOL CASES

Incident: Ashli Babbitt, an Air Force veteran, was shot and killed by a Capitol Police Officer and Capitol Police Officer Brian Sicknick died of injuries sustained on January 6, 2020, at the U.S. Capitol.

Scenario: During the storming of the U.S. Capitol, Babbitt was shot while attempting to enter a secure room. She was admitted to the hospital and died later that evening. She was not armed and there is an active investigation into the shooting. Officer Sicknick was involved in a physical struggle with rioters inside the building where he was reportedly hit in the head with a fire extinguisher. He retreated to the police offices inside the building and later died from his injuries.

Supporters of President Trump gathered in protest outside the U.S. Capitol when the Trump rally "Stop the Steal" speeches were over. There were groups and many unaffiliated individuals attending the protest who entered the Capitol. The individual who struck Officer Sicknick has not yet been identified. The officer who shot Babbitt has been identified as a Lieutenant with the Capitol Police.

After two months of allegations of a stolen election, the counting of Electoral College votes became a flash point for many on the Right. They were fueled by reports of ballot tampering, ballot box fraud, and other election irregularities.

Groups involved: Stop the Steal, Trump supporters, Capitol Police, Antifa, others unknown.

Evaluation: Media outlets and some Democrat politicians have called the storming of the Capitol an attempted coup and an act of domestic terrorism. Calling it a coup is a ridiculous attempt by the Left to elevate the severity of this incident. A coup is an illegal attempt by a small group to violently seize power from the existing government and become the new governing power. Not even a shred of evidence supports the allegation. Riot, yes. Coup, no.

Domestic terrorism isn't out of the question. But it is a hard sell to label the riot at the Capitol domestic terrorism without bestowing the same label on Antifa/BLM after they terrorized 2020. The motivations of those who entered the Capitol will determine whether this was an attempt to violently interfere with the operations of government. That could raise the possibility of sedition charges for anyone found to have attempted that.

Those who broke into the Capitol will likely face federal charges. The person(s) who attacked Officer Sicknick will face murder charges if identified.

The officer who shot Babbitt was acting in an official capacity protecting the people inside the building. An investigation will determine if that action was legitimate use of force based on an imminent deadly threat. Public statements by eyewitness Representative Markwayne Mullin (R-OK) do not seem to support the contention that Babbitt represented a deadly threat.[46]

Implications: The violent seizure of one of the seats of our government is a very uncommon occurrence. It was done in furtherance of a political cause which makes it additionally concerning. The First Amendment only protects peaceable assembly to petition the government for redress of grievances. This was not peaceable and therefore falls under the potential consequences for whatever crimes were committed.

7

THE PRICE OF REVOLUTION

AND THE PATH TO

REDEMPTION

Nothing in this book is legal advice. It is not a DYI on how to start, stop or operate any type of militia, insurrection or terrorist group. Neither does it condone, support or encourage any type of violence. If you find yourself in court and make the statement I read how to do that in Jim Hanson's book enjoy prison, because you're an idiot. Heck, I might even testify against you.

REVOLUTION

Deciding to stage a revolution is exceptionally risky business. The U.S. government has almost all the advantages. It has the military, law enforcement, and intelligence gathering entities. It also has the ability to pressure people into working against a cause or at a minimum not helping.

It is doubtful the government would recognize any grievances presented by revolutionaries as valid. These groups will at best be considered criminals, but more likely be tagged as insurrectionists or domestic terrorists. That means all of the state powers will be arrayed against them.

Law enforcement has many options for dealing with terrorists and insurrectionists under existing criminal law. Basically, everything involved with prepping for a revolution is a crime of some sort. Any time they catch wind of a festering nest of bad intentions they can usually deal with it piece by piece. Many of these enterprises began with big ideas and grand plans but were taken apart by the government's pursuit of the many felonies they commit along the way. They usually end before ever launching their master plan.

The FBI and Department of Homeland Security have well-established programs for investigating and mitigating against domestic terrorism. They monitor all kinds of online media and other recruiting mechanisms. They send undercover personnel to infiltrate whenever a threat escalates to a level to require it.

These together have been tremendously effective at limiting the amount of revolutionary activity in the country to the bare minimum over the years. Recently our streets have been messier than usual. There have not been many times in our country's history when nationwide riots lasted for months at a time. This means stronger measures may come into play.

The trump card possessed by the President in dealing with any type of organized violence is the Insurrection Act. This is what most people refer to as invoking martial law although it does not grant any authority to change laws, just to stop rebellion. It allows active duty military troops and federalized National Guard troops to be deployed inside the United States. This can be in response to an external threat like the drug cartels operating on our side of the Southern border. Or it can be due to an internal rebellion that rises to a level beyond the capabilities of law enforcement.

The authority to use the Insurrection Act lies entirely with the president as Commander in Chief. There is a requirement that a warning to disperse be given to violators, a form of crying havoc prior to letting slip the dogs of war.

The Insurrection Act has been used several dozen times in our history for reasons including suppressing the Ku Klux Klan; unrest following gubernatorial elections; and a number of times for sustained riots. President Trump threatened to use it during the 2020 Antifa/ BLM riots if governors failed to contain them.

TURNING DOWN THE HEAT IN 2021

Limiting the current level of violence must deal with two elements. The first is the violence committed by the Lunatic Fringe on both the Left and Right. These are people outside the bounds of acceptable society attacking because they believe the system that built and runs this country must be destroyed and replaced.

The second is the larger struggle between the Right and Left being waged within the bounds of our political, legal, cultural, and educational systems. Our goal here is to show where some of the extremist elements on both political fronts fit into the definitions of insurgency, insurrection, terrorism, and potentially revolution. Then we need to devise methods to mitigate their violence and influence.

Although the chances of a full-on shooting Second Civil War between Left and Right remains slim, there's unfortunately growing support for the idea. There are groups who actively talk about it and would not be against one. There have always been fringe elements who chattered about or even advocated such a course. Now, like the removal of the Left's taboo on openly admitting their embrace of Socialism, a number of people and groups who condone a civil war who were once reticent to candidly discuss it do so openly.

INSURRECTION, SEDITION, AND DOMESTIC TERRORISM

Those are the major crimes in play when groups are conducting violence in pursuit of political ends. We are not going to make any legal judgments about what the correct application of charges would be. We will examine the correlations between the motivations, goals, and actions of the violent actors in the current unrest and how those match up with some of these terms.

18 U.S. Code § 2383 defines someone guilty of the crime of insur-rection or rebellion as:

> Whoever incites, sets on foot, assists, or engages in any rebellion or insurrection against the authority of the United States or the laws thereof.[47]

18 U.S. Code § 2384—defines seditious conspiracy as:

> If two or more persons in any State or Territory, or in any place sub-ject to the jurisdiction of the United States, conspire to overthrow, put down, or to destroy by force the Government of the United States, or to levy war against them, or to oppose by force the authority thereof, or by force to prevent, hinder, or delay the execution of any law of the United States, or by force to seize, take, or possess any property of the United States contrary to the authority thereof.[48]

Per FBI:

> Domestic terrorism: Violent, criminal acts committed by individuals and/or groups to further ideological goals stemming from domestic influences, such as those of a political, religious, social, racial, or environmental nature.[49]

The first two, insurrection and sedition, involve attempts to sub-vert or overthrow the government. Terrorism is focused on achieving specific changes in policies rather than attacking the government as a whole. Terrorist acts could be used as part of either an insurrection or seditious conspiracy.

Motive matters completely in all of these cases. An attack on a federal building could be simply a case of vandalism. If the goal is to hurt innocents to affect a cause such as police violence then it could be domestic terrorism. For it to be either insurrection or sedition, the goal must be to disrupt, take control or replace the government. The term coup gets bandied about quite a lot and is usually misused. It is not a legal term in U.S. law and the common usage meaning an attempt to overthrow the government is covered by sedition and insurrection.

In addition to properly identifying the potential crimes, we should also consider the repercussions of charging people under any of these three major crime categories. They all carry heavy emotional significance as well as heavy penalties. If they are going to be applied at all in the present climate of simmering conflict, they must be applied equally. The Left doesn't want to charge their compatriots, only people from the Right. That's a huge problem.

One of the biggest frustrations for many on the Right during the sustained 2020 riots was the lack of even the most basic consequences for those responsible. Police forces were often told to stand down and simply allow the rioting to occur. This was especially galling when the rioters literally claimed territory in Seattle and declared their own state. It was allowed to remain for weeks.

After the storming of the Capitol, there was a concerted effort by many to immediately classify it as an act of domestic terrorism, insurrection, or even sedition. The heads of the military services, the Joint Chiefs of Staff, published a letter saying that on January 12, 2021:

> We witnessed actions inside the Capitol building that were inconsistent with the rule of law. The rights of freedom of speech and assembly do not give anyone the right to resort to violence, sedition and insurrection.[50]

Releasing the statement could be seen as undue command influence if any military personnel attended the rally. It was not illegal to attend, only to commit crimes there. And as noted, insurrection and sedition require the motive of overthrowing the government. There was no evidence when they wrote this it was applicable to any of the protestors.

If it is uncovered that any of those who took part in the violence intended per the sedition law:

to prevent, hinder, or delay the execution of any law of the United States, or by force to seize, take, or possess any property of the United States contrary to the authority thereof

. . . then they absolutely should be charged with that crime. If that is not certain, then lesser charges are proper. What is not proper is for the nation's highest military commanders to prejudge this and issue a statement doing so.

CATEGORIZING THE CRIMES

The groups involved in recent violent acts are diffuse and not centrally organized with leaders calling the shots. They are ideologically aligned and have grievances that are somewhat consistent with Antifa and BLM on the Left and Constitutionalist and nationalist movements on the Right. The bad actors committing violence on both sides have a core grievance and also a lot of more diverse issues. But in the recent unrest it was police violence for the Left, and election results for the Right.

For the purposes of this book, we will consider the violent subsets of these groups to be separate from the movements with whom they share some beliefs. The people involved with either of these causes who acted within the boundaries of their civil rights do not share responsibility with those who acted as criminals or worse. Descriptions of the bad actors as related to the larger groups are to allow us to identify their origins and hopefully determine how to stop the violence.

2020/2021 VIOLENCE RESPONSIBILITY

BLM organized hundreds of protests in 2020. It soon became apparent that many of them were launch pads for violence. Those led to the riots which caused billions of dollars in damage and dozens of deaths.

Organizationally they tolerated looting and violence committed by those who shared allegiance to their cause. They also gained leverage in negotiations with the local and state governments in the areas they protested. This was accomplished both through the masses of people they brought and the violence that came along with it.

Antifa has no claim to be a peaceful group. To the extent they organized it was around the idea of overthrowing the government. They used violence as a tool to attack government institutions and to put fear in those who opposed them. They seized an area in Seattle and occupied a police station while declaring themselves the new government. They joined in the BLM protests and often joined with the most radical BLM members to form the core that set off the violence.

Stop the Steal and some related groups organized the January 6, 2021 protest in DC. It brought a large number of people unhappy with the conduct of the presidential election and the lack of resolution of the legal challenges. This is a fully legal form of political speech protected by the First Amendment. The rally they held at the Capitol was not organized in any way that suggested it would be violent, let alone try to overthrow the government. It was attended by a large crowd and the vast majority acted peacefully and properly.

A small number of people, however, came to the event with bad intentions and acted on those. They seemed to be operating on their own or in small unaffiliated groups. They did not appear to have been organized to replace the government. Some did seem intent on disrupting the counting of the Electoral College vote.

CONCLUSIONS

BLM does not openly call for violence but accepts and capitalizes on it to achieve its political goals. The ongoing and consistent appearance of this violence provides value to the group by creating fear among the populace. That creates concern over repercussions by the governments where they operate and often causes them to agree to BLM demands. These are hallmarks of Domestic Terrorism. BLM should be thoroughly investigated to determine potential legal action.

Antifa openly calls for and conducts violence to create fear and achieved a local overthrow of government in Seattle. They are almost certainly a domestic terrorist organization and charged with insurrection and sedition.

Stop the Steal didn't call for violence and the event at the Capitol was the only instance so far where violence erupted. The attempts to use pressure to influence politicians to act and address the issues they raised about the election is fully protected speech.

It is worth watching going forward to see if the Inauguration of Joe Biden as President exacerbates their concerns and if the rhetoric changes to advocating some form of rebellion. Unless that occurs, StS has not shown any characteristics of domestic terrorism, insurrection or sedition.

The people who stormed the Capitol, on the other hand, may have had those intentions. Some of them were simply caught up in the fervor and considered entering the Capitol to be a continuation of their political speech. That is not the case. At a minimum it is trespassing and the federal equivalents. Ironically, they may be subject to increased penalties because of an Executive Order by President Trump in response to the Antifa/BLM destruction of statues and monuments.

Some of them, however, came to DC with the express intention of committing violence. This should be investigated. If they intended to stop the Electoral College activity in Congress or to commit any violence against members of Congress or others in government, that fulfills some of the requirements for sedition. Bringing pipe bombs and other destructive devices could also be considered domestic terrorism.

WHAT COMES NEXT?

The violence associated with these groups requires that we maintain vigilance. The Antifa/BLM riots were successful in many ways and they will be back in destruction mode when future incidents involving police inevitably occur. Antifa has not achieved their goals and are still actively conducting an insurrection in Portland. The large number of people who believe the election was stolen are unlikely to change their minds. The acts of a Biden Administration to push the agenda of the Left will likely fan the flames of dissent and unrest. Bottom line, these problems aren't going away any time soon.

CONSEQUENCES OF INSURRECTION

We have outlined the laws, rules, and precedents that apply when any collection of citizens steps outside the political process to make changes. This was designed to give an overview of the general concepts that govern what is essentially a counter-governmental act.

None of this is crystal clear. I do not accept the common idea that "one man's terrorist is another man's freedom fighter." That conflates motives with tactics. Terrorism is purposeful attacks on innocents and non-combatants. It doesn't matter how righteous they or anyone else thinks their cause is. Attacking innocents makes a person a terrorist. No protections or legal status should apply and the full force of the law should be levied against them.

Even if not attacking innocents, good intentions do not protect these groups. In essence, any acts taken by a group in defiance of the established government are at risk of the punishments under the laws of that government. No one can magically exempt themselves. The United States is a sovereign state as are all the properly-constituted subordinate government entities.

Any person or group that violates the laws of these governments can only expect relief from punishment if:

1. They succeed in overthrowing them or removing themselves from their jurisdiction.

2. They convince law enforcement or the justice system to not charge them.

3. They convince a jury to not convict them.

The first one is not going to be much help unless it involves overthrowing the entire U.S. government. It is hard to imagine a scenario where radicals in say Des Moines, Iowa, execute a coup on their city government and install a revolutionary council. Harder yet to fathom that lasting more than a short time before the state and federal authorities came down on it with irresistible force.

They would certainly avoid consequences if they manage to win their fight. They would also gain the added advantage of history being written by the victors. They could pen heroic tales about themselves and their compatriots. Although unless they had a rock-solid plan for clamping down on freedom of speech and the press, that would not likely go unchallenged for long.

This is by far the least likely outcome of any resistance movement as the odds are overwhelmingly stacked against it. The Civil War is a very painful history lesson on this. Roughly half the country seceded, declared themselves a nation, and put all the industry, resources, and human capital they had into it. The Confederacy was soundly defeated, although at a massive cost to both sides. No modern entity will likely fare any better.

It would take an extraordinary provocation to get to this point again. The likelihood of success would still remain very low. There are occasional discussions about a national divorce or some type of split between Red and Blue America. These have intensified lately and have progressed to come from much more mainstream people. Five years ago, it all seemed like crazy talk. Now we have to entertain the possibility although it is still an extreme long shot.

But we do have groups on both the Right and Left who want to fundamentally transform our government. Currently, there are far too many instances of violence and coercion being used to push for these changes.

The power to arrest or not and to charge a crime or not is at the discretion of law enforcement and officials in the justice system. The only power to convict and therefore authorize the state to dispense punishment lies with the citizenry. It is solidly codified in the Sixth Amendment of the Constitution:

> In all criminal prosecutions, the accused shall enjoy the right to a speedy and public trial, by an impartial jury of the state and district wherein the crime shall have been committed.[51]

The reasons for this are germane to this conversation as they relate to fundamental fairness with the concept of a jury of peers. Crimes should be considered in context by others of similar backgrounds. More importantly, the Founders did not want the state to have any ability to judge the people independently of a final check by fellow citizens.

Jury nullification was considered to be a feature, not a bug in this way. It allowed a jury to decide that even if a member of the community had clearly committed a crime, they were not required to convict them. The overall circumstances could lead members of a jury to agree that punishment was not warranted and essentially overrule the law.

Picture a case where a man's daughter was raped and he later comes upon the villain. He proceeds to administer some rough justice and is apprehended and charged for that. If a jury of his peers doesn't feel punishment is warranted, they can set him free. Even a single jury member can sometimes hang a jury and stop a conviction.

That is a basic check on the power of the state and in a case of insurrection or other uprising against a government it may play a major role.

One more potential liability for those involved with resistance is getting sued. The right to peaceably assemble, speak and petition for redress of grievances cannot be infringed by the government. But, if a person's actions hurt others they may be open to civil action for the damage caused or people hurt.

There is an ongoing case of this related to a Black Lives Matter protest. It was designed to block a highway and then do the usual speeches and chanting. It got violent and one of the rioters hit a police officer in the head with a large rock.

The officer sued the organizers of the event including prominent activist DeRay McKesson saying that because the entire premise of the protest was illegally blocking a highway:

> McKesson breached his duty of reasonable care in the course of organizing and leading the Baton Rouge demonstration...McKesson should have known that leading the demonstrators onto a busy highway was most nearly certain to provoke a confrontation between police and the mass of demonstrators, yet he ignored the foreseeable danger.

That could throw a monkey wrench at civil disobedience which is one of the main components of activism on the Left.

McKesson v. Doe, Doe v. McKesson, 945 F.3d 818 (5th Cir. 2019), *petition for cert. filed*, No. 19-1108 (U.S. Mar. 5, 2020).... a case out of the Fifth Circuit, could not be timelier. It examines whether a protest organizer, racial justice activist DeRay McKesson, can be held liable for injuries that a police officer sustained during a Black Lives Matter protest. The Court should take the case: The Fifth Circuit's holding creates a negligent protest standard, in which protest organizers can be held liable for any foreseeable violence that occurs during the course of the protest, regardless of whether the organizer intended, authorized, directed, or ratified the violent act.[52]

The lawsuit was initially dismissed but a panel on the Fifth Circuit Court reinstated it. This is causing considerable consternation among a wide array of Leftist activist organizations and their supporters. They claim this will essentially limit freedom of speech and assembly by making organizers liable for the illegal actions of anyone who attends even if they did not call for or approve of it.

That is a fair and legitimate argument and it seems likely they will prevail on those grounds. A critical qualifier pertinent to this case is that McKesson explicitly organized the event to be an illegal activity. They claim this is a longstanding tradition of civil disobedience such as protests in the Civil Rights movement—things like Black people going into lunch counters where they were banned from eating.

There's a difference here in that the protesters are not saying the right of way on the highways represent an un-Constitutional affront like segregated lunch counters. They are simply using that illegal activity to gain publicity and attention to their cause. The ramifications of that on the criminal side are again up to the discretion of the police and prosecutors. They decide whether to arrest and prosecute.

The legal options of others damaged in the process of a purposely illegal action are unclear. What if such a case got to a civil trial and the jury members thought about how mad they would be if they were trying to get to work? Or they had seen the footage of motorists being dragged from their cars and beaten by mobs? The jury nullification could just as easily become jury righteous vengeance.

That seems unlikely but the second and third order effects and consequences of planning and conducting illegal activities for political purposes certainly must be considered.

REMOVING YOURSELF FROM JURISDICTION

Another way to attempt to avoid prosecution is claiming the government has no jurisdiction over you in some way. This has been attempted numerous times. In 2014, a Nevada rancher named Cliven Bundy refused to pay increased fees to allow his cattle to graze on federal land adjacent to his property. Bundy and his supporters claimed the federal government was not authorized to administer public land. There was significant legal precedent saying otherwise and this led to a standoff.

The Bureau of Land Management began to round up Bundy's cattle for deportation. Eventually, Bundy and his supporters showed up armed and in force. The local sheriff convinced the Bureau of Land Management to stop the round up. At this point a large array of people and groups occupied the area for several months. Things flared up several times during this with armed protesters and law enforcement in direct confrontation. It never spilled over into active fighting.

Nevada Governor Brian Sandoval rattled a few cages when he spoke in favor of the Bundys regarding the beef (pun intended) with the Bureau of Land Management. He said:

> No cow justifies the atmosphere of intimidation which currently exists nor the limitation of constitutional rights that are sacred to all Nevadans. The BLM needs to reconsider its approach to this matter and act accordingly.[53]

The Bundys and the other groups involved in the stand-off raised numerous claims. One was that the federal government had no jurisdiction. None of their theories about why the government was not sovereign survived legal scrutiny. In the end it became a waiting game.

Eventually the protesters left and the stand-off ended peacefully. The protesters had not achieved their goal of removing themselves from federal jurisdiction. They also did not escalate to armed conflict to pursue that goal. They did avoid arrest and prosecution on some of the potentially most serious charges stemming from when supporters pointed weapons at federal officers. They also escaped many of the charges that were brought in mistrials and hung juries.

Of the three ways to avoid the consequences of an extralegal confrontation with the government, they took advantage of 2 and 3 and avoided major repercussions. They did not in any way advance their claims against federal jurisdiction. The government simply decided to avoid another physical confrontation by not rounding up the cattle and is pursuing the grazing issue in the courts.

REFUSAL TO ARREST OR PROSECUTE

The months of rioting in Portland and the actual seizure of part of Seattle by militants showed what happens when a government with jurisdiction refuses to exercise it. They chose not to enforce lawful control of violent acts or to prosecute them when offenders were arrested.

Anyone contemplating revolutionary activity should be rightly concerned about the powers of government that can be brought to bear against them. Ordinary citizens should also be concerned by some recent examples of government entities failing to properly protect them.

The Department of Justice declared these cities and New York City to be Anarchist Jurisdictions. This was based on an executive memorandum from President Trump regarding their possible loss of federal funding for failure to properly secure their cities.

The U.S. Department of Justice today identified the following three jurisdictions that have permitted violence and destruction of property to persist and have refused to undertake reasonable measures to counteract criminal activities: New York City; Portland, Oregon; and Seattle, Washington.[54]

Seattle became a national spectacle.

Seattle Mayor Jenny Durkan jokingly stated that the area could hold a "summer of love," alluding to a mass gathering of peace activists in 1967 in San Francisco.[55]

What it turned into was chaos and violence. It was a Woke *Lord of the Flies* with the added craziness of warlords handing out AR-15s to random people for "security." After three weeks and multiple murders, the Mayor decided to try governing again and sent in the police to clear out the den of anarchy.

Portland spent months with its local infestation of Antifa and BLM burning and rioting downtown. The Mayor refused to take action beyond purely defensive measures. That led to the federal government sending in units to protect its buildings which were under attack or co-located with the local justice buildings. It was a lawless circus and has still come to no actual resolution.

New York has had plenty of riot problems, but the main issue putting it in the collection of anarchist zones was the decision to cut more than $1B from the police budget. There had already been major cuts to police activity and resources but this was a stunning surrender to the demands of the BLM mob.

Unsurprisingly, the violent crime rate in the city has been skyrocketing ever since the cutbacks in patrols occurred. They gained momentum as criminals learned there was no one out there to rein them in.

THE MILITIA CALLS ITSELF UP

This is an area where the militia as described in the Second Amendment has a historical role. This topic was explored by Dr. Brad Patty in a piece for Security Studies Group called "A Theory of the Militia."

He considered the right of citizens to operate as a militia absent any call up from federal, state or local authorities. The well regulated militia in the Second Amendment is not beholden to any governmental control unless called up by a government entity. The citizens do have a right to essentially self-militia.

> Much more likely is when citizens come under attack by terrorists, insurrectionists, rioters, arsonists, or looters. In that case citizens are very likely to be the only force capable of responding in defense of the common peace and lawful order at least for a short time. In the recent crisis, however, we have seen several occasions when the police force vanished from afflicted areas of cities for the whole night or longer. Citizens who are left to themselves by a failure of state and local power have every right to defend the common peace and lawful order against those who would destroy it.

They have the right to do so, but must accept the consequences of their actions when the government authorities eventually reassert control.

> Ordinary citizens who decide to call themselves or each other up as militia enjoy no immunity for their actions. They are formally held to the law. For those who suggest that police should be stripped of qualified immunity, the citizen-called militia thus offers an option which actually has a higher degree of legal accountability. They can be held strictly to ordinary law, even though they are likely to be acting in extraordinary circumstances.
>
> Note that this may mean that citizens have to defend each other with the jury function. Ordinary self-defense law often does not permit the use of lethal force to defend property. When business owners are facing arsonists or looters and a police response is absent, however, more than private property is at stake. Should a prosecutor fail to recognize that

and bring charges against citizens who use their militia function in this way, other citizens as jurors have the duty to consider whether the state can rightly enforce its laws against the people who defended what the state abandoned. If jurors consider that their fellow citizens used good judgment and reasonable force in the face of the collapse of ordinary law, they should approve the action by acquitting the citizens.[56]

REDEMPTION

The question now becomes how to deal with the elements who will continue to step outside of our political process. One way to frame the problem and some potential solutions is to view these movements as domestic insurgencies.

Per Department of Defense Joint Publication 3-24 Counterinsurgency (COIN):

> Insurgency is the organized use of subversion and violence to seize, nullify, or challenge political control of a region.[57]

The main difference between insurgency and terrorism is the choice of targets and the goal of the movement.

Terrorism is a precursor to and an indicator of the potential for civil war. It is the intentional targeting of innocents to influence the rest of the population and groups or governments the terrorists wish to, well, terrorize.

Insurgencies attack the forces of the government and its assets. The goal is to gain the support of the populace and rally them to the cause. It's important to look at those on both sides who are beyond the bounds of decent and legal behavior.

They often cross over in targeting because they fail to read and heed definitions like this and mostly operate outside law and restraint. That makes it difficult to categorize them as one or the other. Even focusing on their goals, defining their intent is difficult and definitive answers are rarely certain.

We can examine how active insurgency and our response played out in Iraq. It is informative as to dealing with disaffected, violent elements inside the civilian populace.

Al Qaeda fights to punish those who offend their extreme Islamist views. They have repeatedly argued against taking and holding territory. This was a defining argument they had with ISIS that kept those groups from joining forces.

ISIS fought a combined terror/insurgency in Iraq and Syria and won. They ran their Islamic Caliphate as a virtual nation state for several years before the very problem al Qaeda had warned of became apparent. With a fixed address, bombs can come visit and occasionally Special Operations forces and their canine friends do just that as ISIS leader Abu Bakr al Baghdadi found out firsthand. ISIS lost the fight against far superior conventional and Special Operations forces, but even so they made it a long and difficult fight. That was a war, not a counterinsurgency operation, because ISIS had progressed beyond insurgent status.

The sad thing is we had defeated the precursor to ISIS, al Qaeda in Iraq (AQI), during the period of the Surge during the Iraq War. This was actually one of the most successful counterinsurgency operations in modern history.

COIN THEN & NOW

Comparing that situation to the current unrest is not equating the absolute savagery of AQI to the current Antifa/Black Lives Matter rioters or those who stormed the Capitol. It is a look at the structure, goals, support mechanisms, and potential responses a COIN mentality brought to successfully ending the ISIS insurgency. It can help us see how we could effectively use those concepts now. If the comparisons are painful, it's because they are accurate. Sometimes the truth hurts. We will use Antifa/BLM for this comparison to simplify terminology, but it applies in a similar way to the violent extremists on the far Right, as well.

THE INSURGENTS

AQI was a conglomeration of former Saddam regime thugs, local youth with limited economic prospects, and outside agitators from al Qaeda and other Islamist extremist groups.

Antifa/BLM is a conglomeration of national activists, local youth with limited economic prospects, and outside agitators from the suburbs and universities.

AQI was infiltrated among the Sunni minority regions of Iraq and were aggrieved by the actions of the central government and its security forces.

Antifa/BLM is infiltrated among the minority regions of the U.S. and are aggrieved by the actions of the central government and its security forces.

AQI held extremist beliefs and conducted terrorist acts that were abhorrent to much of the rest of the populace. They maintained influence largely through fear of reprisal against any who failed to follow their rules.

Antifa/BLM holds radical beliefs and conducts acts of violence that are abhorrent to much of the rest of the populace. They maintain influence largely through fear of reprisal (violence or cancel culture) against any who fail to follow their rules.

THE COIN APPROACH IN IRAQ

Counterinsurgency is a core Special Forces mission and is often conducted by multiple A teams living with the local populace. They have language skills and build trust through sharing the danger and sacrifice of the people. They train local security units to oppose insurgents using their knowledge and skills; and, access superior U.S. firepower when needed.

In the Surge timeframe during Operation Iraqi Freedom, there was such a large geographical area and population at risk that this mission had to be done by large, conventional units rather than 12-man A teams. The basic concept remained the same.

- Create initial security through application of as much directed force as necessary

- Recruit and train local security forces to enforce it

- Begin economic recovery, education, and advancement projects in the secure areas

- Integrate recovered zones into the larger cultural and government framework

This happened in the Sunni regions with the Sons of Iraq. Formed mostly of military-aged males with no work prospects, it kept them out of the recruiting pool for AQI. It also allowed them to regain their honor with both the work and by keeping their families and communities safe.

THE COIN APPROACH IN AMERICA

- Create initial security through application of as much directed force as necessary. Use local and federal law enforcement assets in concert with prosecutors willing to bring powerful charges to break the backbone of the active violent insurgencies.

- Recruit and train local security forces to enforce it. The local gang-aged males are key. If they become foot soldiers for Antifa/BLM or join criminal gangs, they exacerbate the problem. If they can be coopted to believe they should be making their communities safer, they become the solution. Not an easy task when a culture that glorifies gangs and violence holds sway.

- Begin economic recovery, education, and advancement projects in the secure areas. Security is meaningless without a path to prosperity. Economic development requires security, an educated work force, and business owners comfortable enough with the risk to invest. The riots ran many of the limited number of these people out of business and away from any interest in rebuilding only to be burnt and looted again. That trust must be developed before they will build again.

- Integrate recovered zones into larger cultural and government framework. This is the payoff for the previous hard and dangerous work. Changing a dominant culture that is nihilistic and unsustainable is challenging to do and to sustain. It is vulnerable even once it is accomplished. That was the problem in Iraq. We won the Surge. President Bush defeated the insurgency, but then President Obama pulls us out almost immediately. The central government went back to its evil ways and within a matter of a few years, AQI had morphed into ISIS and millions suffered for our lack of foresight.

COMMON GROUND WITH BLM?

There are certainly elements of Antifa/BLM who deserve to see the inside of a federal prison and not much else, ever. But by and large, they are highly-motivated destroyers of property, not murderers. That means any plan must assume they are integrated back into a community now purged of the most radical elements.

There is considerable overlap between these COIN concepts and the demands of the BLM movement:

> A shift of funding from police budgets into community services and community capital, resulting in a smaller force and more civilian jobs.[58]

Defund the Police was horrible marketing but some of the ideas fit well in COIN:

> Right now, cities across the country are rethinking municipal budgets and reevaluating whether the police are doing jobs they were never intended to do. We have a unique opportunity to cut the spending of police forces that consume ever larger shares of city budgets, producing billions in savings that can be reinvested in a shared vision of community safety, infrastructure, and recovery that does not rely on the police.[59]

COIN TACTICS FOR THE RIGHT

The organizations of the Right have a mixed bag of grievances. The more extreme ones, like the neo-Nazis, are simply beyond the pale and there is no point in even entertaining their sick views. They are a blight on humanity and a problem for law enforcement.

Many of the other groups are disaffected because they don't feel that government obeys the social and legal compacts outlined in our founding documents. In some cases, they have valid complaints while in others they hold views difficult to reconcile with our current culture and society.

One of the most important ideas of our founding was Federalism. This ensures that while the federal government has certain powers and can control some areas of life, the bulk of lawmaking and governing should be done at the state and local level. A government that is closest to its citizens is more likely to be responsive to their wants and needs. The Founders had just escaped religious persecution and were not about to allow tyrannies to develop and destroy their freshly won freedoms.

Federalism allows different states to have different styles and amounts of government. That allows people to choose where they want to live based on the type of governance and the people that attracts. This may not satisfy all of the grievances these groups have, but it allows them more responsive leadership.

Part of applying COIN strategy and tactics to these groups and individuals is getting them invested in the political process not the government destruction process. Love of government is hardly a staple of the Right making this a heavy lift. Part of what Donald Trump brought to the game was a voice for these folks. He was sick of weak, failing, intrusive government, too. He promised to get government off people's backs and out of their lives.

That's the message we must continue to bring. We all have more of a chance to influence things in the direction we want if we are working together. This is not the time for revolution except as a figurative term for major changes to the political and cultural landscapes. That should be something we can join forces over.

8

THE WAR OF IDEAS

THE FORCES ARRAYED in our growing conflict are broadly characterized as Left and Right in American politics. They are often treated as extreme extensions of the Democrat/Liberal/Progressive and Republican/Conservative/Libertarian political spectrum. The analogies break down at the lunatic fringes on each end.

There is little disagreement the country has been moving culturally and politically to the Left for decades. The Counterculture movement in the 1960s fought to overturn the repressive nature of the uptight white guy world of the 1950s.

Civil rights was a major win for all humanity. The fight for equality wasn't drawn on party lines. People on both the Right and Left worked tirelessly to bring about rights that apply to all people equally. The Left seems to have given themselves sole credit that wasn't theirs to take.

One of the many problems with the Left is their inability to be gracious victors. They won the battle for gay marriage, gays in the military, then moved on to transgender men and women not only serving in the military but having their sex change procedures paid for by the military. As usual with the Left, they had no self-control and didn't stop there. They are pushing legislation that makes mistakenly misgendering a person a hate crime. Give them an inch and they take a mile every time.

They have created a system where all things must be equally valued, regardless of whether they are actually good or even make any sense. Well, at least those things they approve of. Not a bad word may be spoken about the secular dogma they call Wokeness.

WOKENESS IDEOLOGY

In order to defeat an enemy, we must understand them. The battle for the Republic pits us against the newest iteration of Socialism, rebranded as Wokeness. Don't doubt for a second it is the same soul and productivity crushing statism that has failed everywhere. A major part of the reason we are discussing this in the context of a Second Civil War is that Wokeness is incompatible with America as we know it. They openly wish to burn it all down and build a new paradise. We are here to make sure they fail.

The American political Left has always had a soft spot for Socialism, they just used to be smart enough to avoid saying it in public. One of the great differences between Left and Right is we believe in individual liberty and they believe in state control. They dislike that people act primarily in their own self-interest and this creates unequal outcomes.

Their plan is to fix that using the power of the state. As Karl Marx taught:

From each according to his ability, to each according to his needs.[60]

The economic and labor prescriptions of Wokeness basically follow the redistributionist plan of Socialism. Kill Capitalism, Eat the Rich and other bumper sticker policies. Then assume that changing the rules of the game completely will have no effect on the way people act. The productive class will just keep over-achieving even though they get no additional value for the effort. This is where the problem of eventually running out of other people's money comes into play as Lady Thatcher pointed out.

The current crop of wannabe tyrants have actually mutated the already awful ideas of Socialism into something worse. They've schemed up an even more invasive agenda to control every aspect of our lives. It makes George Orwell, author of *1984,* about the dangers of totalitarian rule, seem like a slacker. Only in the cocoon of academia insulated from reality could this incoherent collection of thought, speech, and action codes be developed.

Wokeness revolves around a few core concepts:

Identity Politics. Each person is defined by and assigned membership in one or more approved victim groups or oppressor groups. These are based mostly on characteristics like race, gender, social class, or religion.

The crazy thing is these people obsessed about discrimination based on race and sex are dividing us based not on how we act, but by race and sex! It's a complete inversion of Martin Luther King Jr.'s dream that one day his children:

> ...will not be judged by the color of their skin but by the content of their character.[61]

Wokeness demands that everyone must identify and organize into these groupings for the purpose of using supposed discrimination as leverage to obtain power and privileges.

Identifying unequal outcomes. Woke ideology says each approved victim group must have representation that matches their percentage of the population in every aspect of life. If they don't, it's "proof" of systemic oppression or discrimination. Any attempt to identify root causes other than that is called blaming the victim.

This ignores the entire science of statistical analysis which says look at all possible causes of an unequal outcome and then see which ones correlate the most to reality. The problem for Woke warriors is that a root cause analysis often shows that systemic issues are less likely causes than personal choices made by the affected people.

Claiming Systemic Racism is one of the most common tactics of Woke policy. It is effective for a simple reason—the grave stain of slavery and subsequent racist discrimination in this country.

Those are two of the most egregious actions we have taken as a nation. They have been overcome and in the case of slavery at the cost of more than close to a million dead in the Civil War. They remain as a reminder that our history of liberty was not always pure.

They should also remind that since the Founding we have continually moved closer to the ideal that all men are created equal. But they are useful to the Woke brigades to effectively play on guilt and to call anyone who opposes their demands a racist. Calling someone a racist is a powerful tool. Most people in America are afraid to be labeled racist knowing their jobs and safety are in jeopardy by even an unsubstantiated slur. Guilty before proven innocent. So they keep their heads down and don't challenge the Woke agenda.

They demand you agree with them that all instances of unequal outcome for Black people are caused by Systemic Racism. Denying you are a racist is even more proof of your racism, according to Robin DiAngelo, author of the most successful book on this topic, *White Fragility*. She goes even further and claims all White people are racist and America is a White Supremacist nation.

It is an absurd collection of logical fallacies and factual inaccuracies driven by liberal guilt. I wrote a book in response called *The Myth of White Fragility* that exposes the circular reasoning and use of shaming. The Left's goal is to force agreement that America is a fundamentally White Supremacist country and that any disparate numbers in achievement are due to racism alone.

That is a false premise based on faulty science, or honestly no real science at all. Sadly, it has been highly effective in convincing large numbers of people to embrace their invented inner racism. This same idea of unequal outcomes can be used for any approved victim group to claim systemic discrimination at the hands of an approved oppressor group.

Grievance Culture. Approved victim groups are mostly useful to the Woke Left as vehicles to present grievances. Grievances are necessary to obtain concessions, privileges and power.

These wrongs can be examples of unequal outcome as we just discussed. A trick they play is to move the goal posts to create new and more creative grievances when the real ones have been addressed.

No one should dispute that Jim Crow laws mandating segregation in the South were a true wrong. But that was fixed, segregation is illegal. As real discriminatory wrongs were righted, Woke culture invented what they call micro-aggressions. These are supposedly remnants of discrimination that still affect the welfare and success of Black people.

For example, if someone walks into a room with a 2-foot-high afro and someone stares at it, that is considered a micro-aggression. While it is possibly a racist reaction, it is more likely to be normal surprise at seeing a relatively uncommon hairstyle. Fewer than 1% of the population wears this hairstyle and seeing it can trigger a curiosity such as "How in the world does it stay up?"

This is a perfectly normal reaction to something that falls outside the norm and is in no way indicative of racism. Country singer Crystal Gayle famously had hair almost five feet long and everywhere she went got incredulous looks and questions. It's human nature.

Wokeness trains members of approved victim groups to actively seek out and catalog any potential grievance and classify it as discrimination. It's the currency of their movement.

The truly sad thing about wokeness is the need for permanent victims to keep the process going. If they ever actually fix the supposed problems the whole scam would come tumbling down. They are not about to let that happen.

Freedom from offense. One rationale for grievance culture is partly to gain power based on assumed oppression. Another equally powerful reason is the belief that people have a right to be free from being offended. As ridiculous as it sounds, it is a deep-seated principle of Wokeness.

They believe it trumps freedom of speech. It can be comical to watch them screaming "Nazi!" at someone who made the factually correct statement that a man cannot become a woman through the power of thought. It's considered hurtful to inject science into gender alignment. But, they completely miss the irony that calling someone a Nazi is also hurtful. It's OK for the defender of Wokeness to hurl heinous insults and obliterate a person's safe space if that person maintains a belief not sanctioned by the Left.

They have long and constantly expanding lists of things a person can't say or think. They are perfectly happy to have those enforced by any means necessary.

Cancel Culture. One of the preferred methods of executing these thought and speech codes is by launching an outrage mob to force offenders out of the public square, their jobs and even society as a whole.

They have a powerful arsenal to use in these attacks including the media, celebrities, activist groups, Leftist politicians, and the hordes on social media who are always ready to grab torches and pitchforks. They will seize on any transgression and create an outrage storm that destroys people in its wake.

These mobs are brutally effective and they are a weapon used in partisan ways. The Left will always excuse their own side except in the most egregious situations. But let any member of the Right step on any of these land mines and they will be erased.

A perfect example recently was the girl in Virginia who echoed a song lyric containing the N-word while celebrating getting her driver's license.[62] She did this as a Freshman in high school. A mixed-race classmate who saw the seconds long clip saved it until she was a Senior and accepted at University of Tennessee as a member of their national champion cheerleading squad.

He then deployed it across social media and the outrage mongers took it from there. She got the boot and the Woke Mob celebrated taking a scalp. Of course, she made a stupid mistake in doing it, but the punishment is nowhere near fitting of the speech "crime."

On the other side of the political trenches, both Jimmy Fallon and Jimmy Kimmel had dressed in blackface and Kimmel had even used the N-word in a song on a comedy album.[63] They both got to apologize and continue raking in fat satchels of cash. It is a mostly one-way street with Conservatives being the ones pushed onto the off ramp.

Even worse is that the N-word is perfectly acceptable in popular culture as long as a Black person uses it. The obscene irony of institutionalizing a speech code that is only enforced based on skin color seems to escape our social justice warriors. If there is one consistent thing in Wokeness, it's hypocritical inconsistency.

Diversity. The statement that diversity is an ideal that makes all things better is a staple of Wokeness. There is no need to question whether this is actually true, we must simply strive to achieve perfect diversity in all aspects of human existence.

But what does it actually mean? In Woke usage it means all approved victim groups must be represented in every job, organization, or economic class in the same number as their percentage of the population. That is certainly worth considering, but it ignores the fact that not everyone in their groups want to be doing some of those things.

It is commonplace to hear that a certain occupation, say industrial engineering, has too few women. This generates a grievance because this is obviously due to oppression by the patriarchy. Or is it? The question they don't like to ask is "How many women actually want to be industrial engineers?"

If fewer women than men choose that profession, then comparing percentages is not just meaningless, it's foolish. Their goal is not actually to fix things, it's finding unequal outcomes and claiming a grievance then using the leverage to extract concessions. It's a grift of the first order.

Intersectionality. This is one of their crowning achievements. The Left realized at some point their ideology was incoherent. Sometimes the different approved victim groups have goals that work against each other. Sometimes the victims themselves are problematic. What do you do with a Black Transgender Woman when doling out the spoils? Does she get two shares, three shares? Do gay White men get two strikes against them as White and male and one in their favor as gay?

It's complicated. They can't reconcile all that stuff, so they invented intersectionality. This framework is supposed to look at all of the factors such as gender, caste, sex, race, class, sexuality, religion, disability, physical appearance, height, and certainly a bunch of others. Then they create an Interlocking Matrix of Oppression. I really wish I was making that up. It takes a whole lot of liberal education to believe something that silly.

Climate Change. This is one of the super duper serious causes for the Left and they are wound up with all kinds of doomsday scenarios. They seem to forget they've made so many of these claims in the past most of us are unfazed at this point. They have moved beyond Al Gore as the spokesperson. That was smart since his Nobel Prize–winning, fear mongering projections from two decades ago all failed to happen.

Now we are being reliably informed by habitual school delinquent, Greta Thunberg that we are all going to die in the next couple of days unless we kill all the cars and cows. She is joined by Representative Alexandria Ocasio Cortez (D-NY) who added the Green New Deal to the discussion. This eco-fantasy comes with a $100 Trillion price tag and the only things it would do for certain are kill our economy (and the cows) and bankrupt us.

LGBTQIA%$? etc. Wokeness is willing to fight this battle to the last letter in the acronym, which seems to grow daily. It is a major part of the culture war they have been winning. There are legitimate disagreements about gay marriage and other policies, but most people in this country have a live and let live attitude about homosexuality.

But that was not good enough for the Woke folk. They began the acronym extension and pretty soon there were too many alternatives to even fit within the rainbow flag. They literally began building new flags for the non-binary, poly-amorous, pansexuals, and a host of others.

Even after taking into account legitimate religious objections to gay marriage, most people were still willing to live and let live. If a guy wants to wear a dress and call himself Sally, a lot of people, myself included, are willing to call him Sally. And we're fine with the idea that he believes he's a woman. But many perfectly decent people don't think that actually makes him a woman.

The problem they have is changing the definitions of man and woman is something most of the country thinks is unwise. Male and female are tougher to game as they still, for now, have biological definitions based on the role of each in reproductive capabilities. Still, through virtually all of existence man was an adult male and woman an adult female.

But that leaves some people out. So, in another attempt to shelter anyone from getting their feelings hurt, the Left wants to force the 99+% inside the norms to adapt to the 1% outside the norms. It's a painfully difficult task as they try to euphemize away the realities everyone else can see. It leads to tortured descriptions like uterus owners, birthing persons, and attempts to figure out how to recommend women get an annual prostate exam.

There is no reason for discrimination or mean behavior toward people with uncertain or unconventional sexuality. There is also no sense in upending the logical biologically-based systems of an entire culture to try to appease the feelings of the few and make that the norm.

Popular culture. They have long controlled television and movie production and these drive the views that make up our culture much more than laws. Promiscuity, drug and alcohol use, gender dysphoria, and many other destructive things are common. The moron-ification of the American male has long been a theme with the Dad figure usually a dopey loser who constantly screws everything up.

Any idea the Left wants to socialize gets injected into plots in small doses which are increased as our tolerance grows. While they claim that tolerance is a goal of theirs, this is the tolerance of a drug user to a dosage, not the tolerance of rationally considered ideas to a thinking person.

Their "tolerance" is such a one-way street it only applies to the ideas they approve. Look, fruitlessly, for positive portrayals of Christian people on TV or in the movies. You won't find many. Conservatives and their ideas are shown as one step away from goose stepping their way to a Klan rally.

There are good people doing conservative TV and movies, but it is a whispering into a hurricane compared to the deluge of dreck churned out by the Left. Some of this is just appealing to the consumer appetite and lowest common denominator. But they always stick some social justice in with the entertainment.

They want us to hold these "truths" as self-evident, when all that is self-evident is how bat guano crazy the whole woke nonsense is. It gives cognitive dissonance a bad name. They defend their new reality with a ferocity that makes cult leaders jealous.

What about the things we believe that Woke adherents don't like? I mean surely they have the decency to grant that on some things we can simply agree to disagree? Not a chance. That's the thing with zealots, they will not tolerate heretics. The belief systems that built the very foundations they are using to do their fundamental transformations, must now be destroyed.

Not just the legitimately outdated ideas like sexism and racism, but meritocracy, individualism and the entire concept of western civilization must be replaced. However they try to package it, wokeness is just warmed-over socialism with a few whacked out ideas even Marx wasn't willing to throw in the mix.

The stealth infiltration and acceptance of their ideas is a battleground in the culture war the Right has all but lost. I say all but lost because a tremendous obstacle to their cunning plan is the Constitution, that dusty old parchment locked away in the archives that nobody reads anymore. They would love to use state power to enforce their thought and speech codes. That's by far the most effective way to create compliance. Just ask any former Soviet dissidents or current residents of the Chinese Communist gulags.

However, the Founders in their wisdom made the Constitution exceptionally powerful. Since the Supreme Court has a Conservative majority, the Liberals can't just edit it to meet their needs. The current crop of Thought Police would have to amend the Constitution and remove the First Amendment for them to be able to achieve their goals. But that roadblock only protects against government censorship.

The Woke Mob is hell-bent on silencing all forms of dissent wherever they may appear. Conservatives must fight them smartly or we will continue to be marginalized.

THE SMARTER AND STRONGER RIGHT

Branding has never been the strong suit of our team. Mostly because the creative class who specializes in that stuff is largely located in the enemy camp. So, we get stuck with awful offal like Compassionate Conservatism. Although to most people not part of the hipster crowd, Wokeness sounds silly as well. But the Left has celebrities who pitch their silliness so they can make it seem cool to be Woke.

The Right is often referred to as the Party of No. There's a fair amount of truth in that because stopping bad ideas is often more important than coming up with cunning new plans. William F. Buckley Jr. famously said:

A conservative is someone who stands athwart history, yelling Stop.[64]

Not because all change is bad, but because change for the sake of change is bad. There are some things that are just such good ideas and that work so well, we should keep them. That is anathema to the Left as their previous ideological construct Progressivism said by its very name.

KEEPING THE CONFLICT TO A WAR OF IDEAS

There are anti-police sentiments on the far Right that definitely clash with the Blue Lives Matter mentality of the rest of the Right. Likewise, there are anti-government anarchists in the Antifa wing who share none of the love most of the Left has for big powerful government.

The Horseshoe Theory says as you move from the political center you initially spread further apart in beliefs and how to implement them. This is the classic statist vs. individualist split. The belief in less government intrusion and control and more individual liberty is associated with the Right. The government as referee, scorekeeper, and purveyor of free concessions is associated with the Left.

That changes as you get farther around the horseshoe and away from the center on both sides. The beliefs and practices start to converge again. You pass through totalitarian control to pure anarchy and unbridled individual freedom which recognize no man-made entity as their sovereign in any way.

These are the people who do the most damage on both sides and they are not effectively controllable by the less extreme folks at the curve of each side of the horseshoe. The totalitarian and individualist/anarchist wings often have a fairly large overlap and travel in similar circles. This has both advantages and disadvantages for controlling violence.

The historical connections and shared belief systems on both the Right and Left do largely extend out to their own extremes with some mutations. The overlap in membership between the far Right/Left and way-too-far elements of each mean there is some visibility into the most radical elements.

It is also much more common for one disturbed individual to snap and start killing than for a group of even three or more to do so. Usually, the less unhinged members in a group stop the craziness from moving beyond boastful bravado.

The exception to this is the mob mentality we have seen all too much of recently. This actually works in exactly the opposite way and the pounding pulse and excitement of being part of a righteous action overcomes the inhibitions of the more reasonable and actual frenzy ignites.

This mob activity has shown up in the Antifa/BLM riots that have on numerous occasions devolved into violence and have seen a small core of activists, usually the Black Bloc, literally light the fires. This progresses to attacking those deemed enemies who they call Nazis or Fascists in a grotesque misuse of those terms. While there have been a small number of times Antifa and actual Nazis have scrapped, mostly they use the slurs to demonize Trump supporters and in some cases even just those in the general public they find insufficiently supportive of "The Cause."

Mobs have taken to harassing diners at restaurants pressuring them, often with implied or direct threats of violence, to say things like "Black Lives Matter." The irony of a group ostensibly involved in what they claim is Anti-Fascist activism running through the streets breaking windows and beating the undesirables somehow escapes them.

Then the true believers are taught they must convert the unwashed masses. They are also told that failure to believe is proof of actual evil. These ideas of Wokeness are so vital there can be no agree to disagree. Silence is violence. Either join the mob or face its wrath.

This sense of righteousness really is dangerous when paired with a lessening or removal of consequences for violent actions. That was seen in the Floyd riots. The police were forced to pull back or out in many cities and the mob saw the vacuum and advanced.

It may require some compromise and new tactics and techniques for police to deal with these activist riots. But there is no incentive for the rioters to change tactics when they get a personal satisfaction out of "punching Nazis" and in many cases the powers that be cave to their demands. It's a perfect situation for them.

The creation of a "police as the enemy" movement is not new, but it was never this widespread or accepted. And this is in a time when police violence against civilians is at an all-time historical low. We have a fervent movement that truly believes the police are a racist and oppressive blight on the country. They continue to demonize the police. But those same police continue to serve the public and give us record lows for violent crimes.

Since the BLM riots began, those cities that followed their prescriptions for cutting police funding and presence have seen their violent crime rates skyrocket. They vilified the police as the instigators of the violence and then refused to let them do their jobs. This paved the way for bad guys to do bad things.

This gets tied in with the idea that Systemic Racism causes the disparate amounts of crime and subsequent numbers of Black prisoners. This is actually reality flipped on its head. Police aren't the cause of the crimes they protect against but that's the story these days. Crime is the real cause of the police activity and therefore the disparate outcomes. But that goes counter to the BLM narrative and is deflected by calling it victim blaming.

If you are willing to go all the way down the rabbit hole with the BLM reasoning, then basically all the pathologies in the Black community are remnants of slavery and continue due to systemic racism. Consequently, making bad life choices isn't their fault, it's ours. Even the violent crimes of the drug gangs are not their responsibility because they only chose that lifestyle due to lack of good options.

There is some truth in the idea that cycles of poverty and violence create a pipeline to prison that is near impossible to escape. The facts show schools in poor Black neighborhoods are substandard and there is little industry or commerce in those communities to provide good jobs. What they don't show with anywhere near the certitude the activists claim is that systemic racism is the sole or even primary cause.

This also infantilizes Blacks by removing responsibility for choices they make as if they aren't capable of making decisions for themselves. The number one predictor for success of a child in America is an intact or two parent household. This is not an opinion; it's a verifiable fact.

Black children are by far the least likely to grow up with that advantage. The extremely personal decision to get pregnant or father children without giving them that advantage is not something the system or racism is causing.

That is a cultural shift in the Black community that is terribly damaging. It stems at least in part from the well-meaning efforts of Liberals. The welfare state they created was meant to ensure a safety net for the least fortunate. It ended up facilitating the ability for fathers to avoid responsibility for children they helped bring into this world. The law of unintended consequences doesn't care about the desire to make the world a better place.

Changing the mentality and cultural acceptance that allows men to father children but avoid responsibility for their care will not be easy. But turning a blind eye doesn't help. This is a massive roadblock to a child's future success and simply giving everyone an out by blaming systemic racism fixes nothing.

THE BLOWBACK FROM THE RIGHT

Differences of opinion about root causes or policies doesn't constitute racism. Conservatives are equally as committed to supporting equality and eradicating discrimination, but the Left has pushed the narrative that the Right wants to keep minorities down.

This cultural shift in personal responsibility has upset many on the Right. The changes we have made toward being a society that lives up to the founding claim "all men are created equal" are unquestionably positive. The lunatic fringe may still try to propagate racism, sexism and xenophobic beliefs, but they don't gain much traction and end up isolating themselves.

A major disagreement between Left and Right is what to do when disparities of outcome that affect their list of approved victim groups are identified. The Left takes these disparities and attaches a claim that some -ism is causing them: Racism, Sexism, Homophobia(ism).

White patriarchal dominance is a historical accuracy in American society. It is equally factual it has been systematically dismantled over the course of our growth as a country. The disagreement is over where do we stand now as far as equal treatment under the law and in the systems and institutions that run our country.

The ascendance of BLM has made race the test bed or battleground for this fight. It has the strongest standing as an issue because no other grievance can compare to the grotesque nature of slavery. The current conflict over the existence of, or lack of, systemic racism also includes the larger notion that the other identity groups have similar claims that must be addressed.

The grievance for many on the Right is these instances of disparate outcome do not by themselves constitute proof of a systemic problem. My book, *The Myth of White Fragility*, covers this in depth. It looks at claims the United States is so infected with Systemic Racism that it is a White Supremacist nation and therefore all White people are racist since they benefit from this.

This line of reasoning is widespread and grew out of Critical Race Theory in academia. Now it is considered a part of diversity and inclusion training at many corporations, schools and even government agencies. It was revealed that training at Sandia Labs, a government research facility, was using this material. This led President Trump to issue an "Executive Order on Combating Race and Sex Stereotyping" which states:

This ideology is rooted in the pernicious and false belief that America is an irredeemably racist and sexist country; that some people, simply on account of their race or sex, are oppressors; and that racial and sexual identities are more important than our common status as human beings and Americans.

It goes on to ban training based on this ideology:

Therefore, it shall be the policy of the United States not to promote race or sex stereotyping or scapegoating in the Federal workforce or in the Uniformed Services, and not to allow grant funds to be used for these purposes. In addition, Federal contractors will not be permitted to inculcate such views in their employees.

This ban is not limited to just Critical Race Theory but written to mirror the equal protection language in the Constitution and also in the Civil Rights Act of 1964. The Executive Order calls for an evaluation of whether this training is grounds for lawsuits.

> Sec. 8. Title VII Guidance. The Attorney General should continue to assess the extent to which workplace training that teaches the divisive concepts set forth in section 2(a) of this order may contribute to a hostile work environment and give rise to potential liability under Title VII of the Civil Rights Act of 1964.[65]

The biggest mistake by proponents of Critical Race Theory and anti-racist training was overstepping and instituting a new form of racial discrimination as the supposed remedy for the kind outlawed 55 years ago. Categorizing all White people as racist based on the color of their skin is, in fact, racist. The theory and training also suffers from a major flaw in its main proposition about Systemic Racism.

The entire game is based on identified disparate outcomes for Black people—such as Blacks are 2.5 times more likely than Whites to be in prison—then claiming this is proof of Systemic Racism that must be addressed.

That is an improper use of statistics. When examining the potential cause of higher incarceration rates, the fact that Black people commit four times the number of violent crimes than White people must be acknowledged. Violent crimes come with prison sentences and this obviously explains a portion of the disparity.

The activists do not want to look at root causes, they simply want to promote the narrative that Black people are victims of White racism. Holding violent criminals accountable for their crimes shifts the blame dynamic away from the broader White community and back to the person who committed the crime. This personal responsibility doesn't perpetuate the systemic racism theory and, therefore, it is racist to even contemplate the idea.

It is easy to see why such an offensive and factually deficient smear causes enormous discontent among the population accused of it. It is wrong and ironically completely racist.

There was a hesitance among many on the Right to engage in arguing about racial issues because being tarred as a racist was often a career-ender and made them a social pariah. The demagoguing has reached such epic proportions, however, that much of the sting is gone. When a major concept in racial politics on the Left literally says "All White people are racist," who cares?

A side bonus of over-using the racist smear is now necessary arguments that had been pushed aside can regain footing and actually happen. The treatment of racial issues as a third rail helped many false ideas to flourish, chief among them is that America is a White Supremacist nation.

Of course, racism still exists here. It exists everywhere in the world. It is a blight of the human condition. But it is not the pervasive, damaging, ever-present boogeyman the Left wants us to believe. They have been gas lighting White people into admitting personal racism toward Black people and groveling apologetically. Watching Antifa/BLM mobs force law enforcement leaders to literally lay down in the streets during riots and protests was obscene. Mobs screamed obscenities and threw things at them, showcasing the fanatic fury of the Left.

There was a heavy reluctance to even express a dissenting Conservative opinion until just recently. It is still risky and can carry a heavy pricetag. Unfortunately, not hearing effective counterarguments paired with the Liberal indoctrination done in schools has led to many people truly believing the hype.

It was painful for Conservatives to be declared racist when many of us have dedicated our lives to making the world, and this country, fair and just place for everyone regardless of race, sexual orientation, religion, etc. It creates a cognitive dissonance that leads to righteous indignation and outright anger.

The Left demands safe spaces free from anything that gives them bad feelz while they continue to actively create a hostile environment for the Right.

THE LUNATIC FRINGE

Biases, bigotry, and other unsavory beliefs are mainstays of fringe groups. The Left's condemnation of America as a White Supremacist country is good in their view. Their reaction is often "If only!" They see this country as dominated by the Left and in thrall to political correctness and reverse racism. As heinous as the actual racist groups are, the Critical Race Theory garbage actually makes them feel their irrationally evil mindset is justified.

The inhabitants of the lunatic fringe on both sides of the political spectrum aren't the best and brightest. They are more like the dumb and dumber. In many cases, they are exact duplicates of the caricatures used to demonize them. Skinhead thugs hating on everyone different than themselves and wild-eyed anarchist freaks burning and beating.

It is nearly impossible to salvage the human decency of those lunatics who are already that far around the bend. But at least their outrageousness makes them easy to track and their diminished intellects make them easier to infiltrate with informants. They are the most susceptible to the counter-extremism tactics that law enforcement has in its arsenal.

It is those people on the next step up the ideological food chain who are the real problem. There are very smart and well-educated people on both extreme ends of the spectrum holding better-defined but often more dangerous beliefs. They aren't ranting and shrieking so they don't immediately set off the whack job alarms. They insulate safe spaces for ideas that metastasize into extremism.

They pose a greater threat and are far more difficult to identify and deal with. Stopping them is one of the keys to ensuring that the internal Cold War here in America doesn't escalate into a full-on civil war.

PART III

THE PATH TO VICTORY

(2021 & ONWARD)

BOTTOM LINE UP FRONT

The 2020 Elections were a debacle in many ways. But they showed that while many Americans did not want a second Trump term, many fewer wanted what the Democrats were selling. The down ticket results gave Republicans a gain of 10 seats in the House of Representatives and significant gains in votes from Blacks and Latinos.

That is something we can build on.

The Woke Mob has driven off many from the previously core Democrat constituency of working people including minorities. They had their livelihoods destroyed by the policies of the Left. As members of the productive class, they believe you should reap the benefits of your own hard work. Many of these people see the degradation of our culture as a corrosive thing as well. They believe in God and family and personal responsibility. They want to be part of a team that values those things. They are perfect additions to expand our team.

But the war is still on and we are still losing. The upside is we have an identified enemy who has shown the threat they represent. We have also seen that people will respond to a rallying cry to defeat it. The key is to build a new infrastructure and platforms for the Right that help in the current fight. The failed establishment institutions that supported the Ivy League, country club and board room agenda of losing gracefully must be upgraded to reflect our new fighting spirit.

It is hard to feel positive in our current situation. But we can present a path to security and prosperity based on the timeless concepts of liberty and responsibility. They have always worked and make a great contrast with the oppressive state control and political correctness of our opponents. That gives us a reason to be optimistic.

We must work to give the angriest elements in our camp productive outlets or we risk any violence they conduct being used to smear the entire movement. The danger is real and a large swath of the movement is not willing to move forward without some retribution. We need to make sure that retribution is figurative not literal.

The path to victory is not violence, it's making sure we have the right forces and resources in play. We control many state governments and it's time to change all the election rules to ensure that every vote is validated with real identification. We must scrub election rolls and stop ballot harvesting. And we must do all of this before the next elections are held because most of the courts ruled that you can't just challenge the rules after you lose.

We must also find a way to keep our tent as large as possible. Many of the Never Trump ilk have permanently exiled themselves and good riddance. But we cannot afford to see a split between the Fighting Right and the Establishment. Both represent a considerable portion of our constituency. We can't leave the party and platform in one group's hands alone. We must place the current danger and our common enemy above internal disagreements and build a better team together.

9

THE RESURGENT RIGHT

THE RIGHT MUST DEFEAT AN IDEOLOGY that wants to replace the Founding ideas of individual liberty and freedom with state control of our lives. That requires a new way to think and talk about ourselves. Our core beliefs and principles will remain the same, but the policies and messages need to match our new challenges and challengers.

The Left believes America today is a wicked place so infected with systemic racism, sexism, homophobia, and other ills they must destroy it to save it. They have been very successful in spreading those ideas even though they are mostly false. Much of what we must do will be information warfare to counter their propaganda. We also need a modern philosophy to give ourselves the moral and political high ground.

America's founding was imperfect. We failed to immediately deliver on the promise that all men were created equal. We must openly admit that. The Left fails to acknowledge the ongoing forward momentum we have made since in delivering it. We can call them out for that. We have continually bent the arc of the moral universe toward justice. But we must also acknowledge that our work is not done yet.

The Left is incapable of moderating its tone in response to this progress. They believe America is evil in the same way Christians believe the devil is. They have substituted progressive ideology for religion in their mindset. It has a dogma and canon and must be accepted without reservation. Join and actively worship with them or be shunned as a heretic.

Believing in God is a sure way to get in their crosshairs. The religious backbone of the Right has always been a strong part of our defense and we must make sure to defend it. It also serves as a counterpart to the morality-free world they want to bring to fruition.

They have become victims of their success and emboldened to believe they can force their agenda on us. But it includes far too many elements that are anathema to normal Americans and counter-Constitutional. Their insularity and confirmation bias have made them immune to seeing the absurd nature of the Woke movement. That absurdity is what we differentiate ourselves from.

SAME PRINCIPLES, FRESH PHILOSOPHY

We need a post-Trump platform and ideology that can unify the MAGA crowd with establishment Republicans and create a governing majority. It must also reach those who may be part of the Democrat constituency now, but who share our belief in hard work, personal responsibility, and individual liberty.

None of these ideas are new, but the circumstances we find ourselves in means we must actually teach many younger Americans what the Founders meant. We must explain federalism, the Electoral College, and in many cases the actual meaning of the Bill of Rights. We need to show why capitalism is not simply heartless. We must fully debunk the idea that if we just inundate the rich with taxes, everything else will work out.

The current divisive climate and unrest may actually be the most fertile ground for such a project in decades. The Left had been making a slow motion move toward a Socialism they wouldn't name, and it was working. They became so enraged by the Trump presidency, they replaced stealth with revolution in the streets. That may turn out to be their fatal mistake. Most Americans were too busy living normal lives to get riled up at every change the Left slipped past us. That's changing. People are paying attention now.

Gay marriage and gays in the military are good examples. Both were issues where valid expectations for equal rights and legal protections rapidly slippery sloped to transgender men can have babies and misgendering someone becoming a hate crime. That took barely a decade. This shows that the threat is real and the time to draw the line is now. We can define a philosophy of actual tolerance for other people that doesn't require upending biology and common sense. Tolerance also means the Left owes society the protected right to express disagreement with their ideas free from fear of retaliation or being canceled.

The bonus from all the Woke Mob riots is that normal Americans could no longer ignore this. People were dragged from their cars and beaten or shot. Billions of dollars in damage was done and much of it to small business entrepreneurs who represented all of us. Watching cities being destroyed as the Democrat leaders refused to let the police intervene were watershed moments. Life under Democrats means the mob rules.

That has led to a much-needed backlash and the current opportunity to build a coalition of the Normals. The Left showed its hand and it's full of jokers. They openly call for the destruction of what they call a White Supremacist country. The rest of us know it as America, Land of the Free.

This new Conservative ideology and platform should not consider race or religion or sex or any other personal characteristic or choice to define an individual in their public life. Those things can mean as much or little as a person wants in their private world. But as a citizen of this country, one is first and foremost an American. The same rights and opportunities must apply equally to everyone. What you do with them is up to you and your success is driven by your skills and effort. Your outcome is uncertain, but it is 100% yours to mold.

VIVE LA DIFFÉRENCE

Donald Trump was the only Republican who could have beaten Hillary Clinton. Whatever else he did, he secured three Supreme Court seats and filled over two hundred federal judgeships with actual Conservative jurists. That gave us at least a generation or two to stop the steep slide to the Left. But he didn't unite even the Right, let alone the country. It's time to look at alternatives and also to accept that the country may not be united any time soon.

The first thing we need is a good way to contrast ourselves with our opponents, and they are doing that for us brilliantly. The Democrats are being led right now by the bat guano crazy wing of their party and an important rule of conflict is:

Never interrupt your enemy when he is making a mistake.

—SUN TZU AND NAPOLEON BONAPARTE

That's not to say there is no support for their slide toward socialism. Bernie Sanders was pulling one-third of the vote in their primaries and their loudest voices are those who share the Wokeness and Social Justice agenda. The Squad dominates the airwaves. It's a group of six egregiously Woke members of the U.S. House of Representatives: Alexandria Ocasio-Cortez (D-NY), Ilhan Omar (D-MN), Ayanna Pressley (D-MA), Rashida Tlaib (D-MI), Jamaal Bowman (D-NY), and Cori Bush (D-MO).

There's a yawning gulf between one-third of the Democrat primary crowd and a governing majority in this country. Their anti-American sentiment, support of violence, and outright crazy ideas like Defund the Police and the Green New Deal make it easy for most people to see them as not just foolish but downright dangerous.

We need an appealing alternative. Marketing has never been the strength of the Right, but we can start with "Not That." Then add that while the country can always use some improvement, we don't need to burn it all down. We can make the conservative case for not fixing what ain't broke.

We can recommend taking a good look at root causes before we go "fixing" disparate outcomes for Black people based on unproven ideas like Systemic Racism. We can propose an education system that teaches real world skills not radical Leftist ideology. We can promise that hard-working people will see the rewards they earn and those who are unable to help themselves will get the help they need. We can promise real tolerance of different lifestyles and beliefs, without a requirement to bow to the politically correct idea du jour or be canceled.

There is a hunger for a reasonable alternative between the polarized camps at either end of the spectrum. Let's give them one.

A NEW COALITION ON THE RIGHT

This philosophy melds the conservative principles that have served us so well for centuries with a modern Libertarian style. We think people should have the legally protected right to live as they wish as long as they aren't harming others. It also needs to incorporate the fighting attitude the MAGA wing has brought to our side. And let's make sure to invite our new friends who used to be Democrats to this party, and our party, too. Many of them no longer recognize the Democrats as the home of the working folks it used to be.

There has not been a strong ideology paired with a positive message from the Right that has resonated since President Reagan. He clearly and powerfully articulated the things about America that lift all of us up and created that "Shining city on a hill." More importantly, he talked about why they were still relevant. This was a clear contrast to the malaise and "America must be transformed" view of President Jimmy Carter and the Democrats. Back then, they promoted many of the policies the Social Justice mob is actually pushing today.

Reagan showed that Conservatism is not simply a refusal to change, it's a refusal to change things that work. That is the kind of revival on the Right we need today. There is a significant amount of tolerance on the Right. It's just the live and let live kind and that drives the activist Left crazy.

They don't want people to make their own decisions because they don't like the decisions people make. Especially when Conservatives ignore their commandments like: Cows and cars will kill the planet; you must recognize however many genders we proclaim today; oh, and by the way, you're a tremendous racist and we demand that you bend the knee and atone for your sins.

That desire to control the masses is deeply ingrained in the Socialist Left and is fundamentally at odds with the Declaration of Independence and the Constitution. Large masses of people in our camp, and many who should join it, still believe the principles of individual liberty and responsibility apply. In a stunning display of political judo, the Left brands this as intolerance.

The question becomes how do we flip that back to its proper perspective and make tolerance for different views the norm again? The answer is: it ain't gonna be easy. Now is a great time to start because the other side has lost its ever-lovin' mind and is giving us the perfect oppressive alternative as a contrast. Act now or they win.

The Left's refusal to allow people to remain neutral helps us recruit for our team. We must have a clear alternative and a positive message. The alternative piece is easy— personal liberty, security and prosperity. Those also go a long way toward the positive message aspect, too.

The Left's relentless messaging of Systemic Racism has put a legitimate fear in many people's minds about being associated with the Right in any way. That is why the silent majority, or at least plurality, was used to describe Trump supporters. But for the Right to succeed, we must grow beyond Trump and remove that fear.

THANK YOU PRESIDENT TRUMP, WE NEEDED THAT

President Trump was the right man for a job we desperately needed done, defeating Hillary Clinton. He did and we all can thank him for keeping us out of her re-education camps.

He stood for a return to many things that have made America great, but not as part of a broader movement that can create a governing coalition. He channeled a properly angry reaction to the oversteps of the Left. He paired that with a promise to fight back against their attempts to fundamentally transform this country into something the Founders wouldn't even recognize. It worked, but it can't work in the long term because it was too dependent on Trump as the ringmaster.

He was a charismatic leader. His rise and election to President showed that the version of Republican politics in play for the past several decades was not acceptable to the majority of available Conservative voters. They had seen cycle after cycle of tough talk and grand promises during campaigns, but business as usual back in Washington after the elections.

There was a distinct and accurate impression that Republicans were letting the country slowly slip away to the Left. The politicians didn't seem to care as long as they maintained their power. The Republican mentality seemed to embrace "Maybe a little bit less of that crazy stuff," but not a hardline, principled stand and certainly no willingness to fight aggressively or risk anything. Just go along get along and keep their waning influence intact for as long as possible.

That all came to a screeching halt in 2016 when America elected a guy who said, "Enough of this garbage, let's fight back." That was what I heard from the first Trump supporter I talked with early in 2016 during the campaign. I explained, "There's no way he can get elected, too many attack points, too much craziness, they'll destroy him in the press." She said two words, and they are the two that changed everything, "He fights."

That's what the large number of Trump supporters who had stayed out of politics wanted. They were sick of getting lied to by politicians who went to Washington and turned into Democrat Lite. Then got rolled over on all the issues they had campaigned on. Trump offered a clear alternative.

But now he must play a new role and neither the establishment wing or the MAGA forces will be in charge. We have to find a way to operate together. We have to be able to disagree on some things and still band together against our common foe.

THE PARTY OF TOLERANCE

The new Conservative philosophy needs to remember that "Politics is downstream of culture" as Andrew Breitbart so perfectly put it. And our culture will deliver what the Left claims—tolerance and inclusion—but without those silly speech codes and wealth redistribution.

We will reach out to all Americans regardless of race, creed, religion, gender, and so on. We will focus on the content of people's character and their willingness to be part of a community that values productivity and competence. One that also recognizes the less fortunate must be taken care of, but social services should be a safety net, not a sustained way of life over generations.

The Social Justice crew is obsessed with Identity Politics and ruling people based on which identity they are assigned or identify with. It's a truly incoherent concept as there is no way to unify a collection of groups that have nothing in common other than grievances against what they perceive as the current system.

It falls apart when they find out the grievances can't all be reconciled and the victim groups have conflicting goals. Circular firing squads form and they commence to eat their own. Again, this is to our advantage as the various groups become more strident and demanding, especially when they are scrapping with other groups for their share of the spoils. The Left believes they can loot America and reward all their client victim groups. That is destined to fail, we just need to help.

How can we do that? Let's start with a positive message and some air cover from the bad example of marauding SJW shock troops. If we can show that Liberalism is intolerant and Conservatism is the actual tolerance, then we have a promising message. But that is just a band aid on a sucking chest wound. We need to take a page out the Left's playbook and change what we know are broken systems that work against us.

We will lose catastrophically if we don't provide an alternative to the pre-school through post-graduate Leftist indoctrination that passes for an education system. The past several generations have been taught America is evil. Today's youth wholeheartedly think they are culpable unless they help destroy this country and replace it with a Woke paradise. They have created a perfect example of the quote from Reagan,

> It's not that our friends on the Left are ignorant, it's that they know so much that isn't so.

We can't put our children into that meat grinder and expect anything back other than vegan tofurkey sausage. We must have an alternative education system and one that focuses on real world skills, not invented social engineering and mind control.

This is another great place to differentiate ourselves from the Wokeness brigades. We believe in people working to produce things or services of tangible value and then exchanging their labor for like value, i.e., the productive class. The Left believes in creating a technocratic and bureaucratic class to rule the rest of us. That cohort ensures we do and think only things they sanction and then they will divvy up and pass out the loot, i.e., a parasitical ruling class.

They absolutely want to get to "From each according to ability, to each according to need" and some of them even say so out loud. The smartest among them couch it in the terms of helping the less fortunate. In the end, it's still just a new flavor of Socialism and destined to destroy the very productivity they want to use to fuel their machine.

They ignore that when they take more and more from people who are successful, those people don't just smile and say "thank you sir may I have another?" Instead, the productive people stop producing. Those people are our base, they are our compatriots, and they deserve the opportunity to enjoy the fruit of their labors. And the freedom to decide how they want to use it to benefit themselves and others.

This split is like the delineation outlined in *Atlas Shrugged* by Ayn Rand. An extreme melodrama for certain, but it defined a very stark and compelling divide between the producers and the looters and moochers. It provides clear insight into being a productive member of society (the Right) or a looter and moocher (the Left).

CHALLENGE ACCEPTED

Conservatives should have the right to educate our children in accordance with our beliefs; refuse to join in what the Left deems as politically correct orthodoxy; and, of course, to think and say things that some people dislike.

It seems crazy to have to lay those things out as a new platform. But can anyone argue that we don't have to claw back control of these things? We are close to losing the culture war which makes our effort a counter-revolution. Accepting this lets us grasp the enormity of the task ahead. Liberals spent the last century building the state and cultural apparatus that currently exists. We must begin a similar task or we will simply be managing the decline.

The advantage we have and have always had is Conservative values are the foundation of the best ideas. Personal liberty and free markets are better for all people than state power and thought police. We have just always suffered from the problem best described as "Democrats are giving away ice cream and Republicans are selling broccoli." Their bumper sticker sloganeering is vastly superior to ours. Their problem is we've all seen Democrat control of cities and states for long enough to prove Liberal results are abysmal.

The targets of our counterattack are many of the same institutions the Left coopted while we were winning the Cold War. We had our eyes on another prize, but the real danger is now inside this country and we must treat it with that same diligence and focus.

10

THE COUNTERATTACK

WE CAN'T JUST BE THE PARTY of opposition to Socialism. We must oppose it, but that alone can't define us. We must rally around central themes essential to maintaining our American freedom, security and prosperity. Here are some foundations for that.

FREEING SPEECH IS THE TOP PRIORITY

We will not be able to win this fight if no one can hear us. That is the Left's plan and it is working stunningly well. We must fight back and break their control of our right to speak freely.

The Constitution forbids the government from abridging freedom of speech, but it says nothing about the Woke Mob and Cancel Culture destroying someone when they don't like what you say.

Cato Institute Poll: 62% of Americans Say They Have Political Views They're Afraid to Share.[66]

Saying the wrong thing today gets people fired, shunned, or worse. This has rightly been the case for dangerously extreme views, but it has become perilously common in the past few years for mainstream Conservative views to also be attacked. The Wokeness doctrine believes that people should be free from being offended. This is fundamentally at odds with the Constitution that firmly enshrines the right to offend in the First Amendment. It is also at odds with the idea of free speech as a component of our society completely detached from the government.

The biggest villains in this are social media giants Facebook, Twitter, Google, Instagram, and YouTube. They now control a distressingly large portion of our shared information space, where we gather to share information and opinions. They are in virtual lockstep regarding censorship of speech they dislike.

These same people are almost entirely consumed with the Wokeness movement and they see their control of our information space as not just an opportunity to end "offensive" speech, but a calling to do so. For them it's a feature not a bug.

The political Right is firmly in the crosshairs of the Thought Police. While they have begun with the more extreme versions of speech, do not for a second believe they will not get to you, too. If you're reading this, you are probably too extreme for them. We can't win the long war without prevailing over this mass silencing of our voices.

Government intervention or control of private actions is something Conservatives instinctively oppose. It is rarely the best way to effect positive results. We limit it to only those things that can't be done any other way. But, and it's a big but, isn't making sure we have free speech one of those things?

That doesn't mean we should want the government to regulate social media, but limiting the tech giants' ability to silence Conservative voices is a much different thing. We can either make sure all viewpoints are welcome or they should feel the boot of the government on their necks.

The tech giants have such near-absolute control now that it is almost impossible for rivals to displace them. This mirrors the situation when just a few companies owned all telecommunications or when electricity was only available from a particular provider. The government didn't allow them to refuse service simply because the owners or their Board of Directors disagreed with the political beliefs of their customers. Yet that is exactly what is happening right now. Conservative thought is actively discriminated against and Conservative thinkers disadvantaged.

Ideally, the tech firms would act as they say they do: They would fix their policies and promote equality. They would control their employees who make decisions about elevating and minimizing Conservative content. But don't hold your breath.

The tech giants claim they are operating with the best intentions. They think stopping "hate speech" is a noble pursuit. They made themselves judge, jury, and executioner empowered to decide what is or isn't acceptable. If they were simply private companies with limited operational span and openly stated their Wokeness-driven terms of service, that would be one thing. But monopolizing the marketplace of ideas while claiming equality and concurrently shutting down Conservative viewpoints is something else altogether.

When they became the sole purveyors of the public information space, their responsibilities changed. There were no alternative places to reach large swathes of the American people and consequently their right to have absolute control should be limited. They are essentially a vital commodity like electricity or water for business or politics or just personal exploration. Google tells you what reality is when you ask it for information. Right now, you might as well be sending that request to the Ministry of Wokeness or to the Priests of the Temples of Syrinx who said in the Rush rock anthem *2112*:

> We've taken care of everything, the words you read, the songs you sing, the pictures that give pleasure to your eyes.

In the end of that epic, the intrepid rockers tear down the temples and state, "We have assumed control." Well, people it's time for us to assume control.

We won't get any reasonable relief from a Biden Administration. They hate the tech firms but for a totally different reason: In a remarkable show of staying on brand it's for not censoring us enough. They don't want a marketplace of ideas, they want government-sanctioned, Wokeness-approved speech codes.

Here's how we take them on.

Antitrust laws are one obvious way to deal with abuses. There is already a case filed by the Federal Trade Commission against Facebook:

> to undo and prevent its anticompetitive conduct and unfair methods of competition...[67]

That's a good start since Facebook controls a massive portion of the online advertising marketplace and they ruthlessly keep other firms out of their digital backyard. The Biden Administration may even continue to push this case even though it began as a Trump initiative. They want leverage against Facebook so they can push them to be even more discriminatory and biased in their censorship. Any pressure on these behemoths now is good pressure as it puts them off balance and on the defense.

Next we attack them with legislation and lawfare in a death by a thousand paper cuts. We have control of a large number of state legislatures with Republican governors and Attorneys General. Most states also have versions of antitrust laws based on the federal statutes. An enterprising state Attorney General could use these to try to open up the field to competition.

A more likely way to gain relief will probably come from consumer laws. This will be a nice way to use the many laws and regulations mostly brought into play by the Left to push back at nasty corporations. We can use them to force their Silicon Valley allies to play fair.

The social media companies all claim they don't discriminate on the basis of political or religious beliefs. But they all do. That opens them up to accusations of not acting in good faith or in accordance with their stated rules and terms of service. Lawsuits can be filed by people whose businesses or other activities were damaged through the unfair application of these rules by the tech firms.

Currently, they suppress or outright ban content and accounts with almost no transparency. They won't say why and give no recourse for those who have their social media existence taken away. If a business owner loses a social media account they worked to build over an issue of personal speech, then the burden to prove that should be on the tech firm not the customer. Lawsuits alleging damages to businesses and reputations based on this could be filed in a number of states.

Consumer protection laws could also be beefed up and modernized to reflect the broad use and necessity of social media accounts. The account holder could be deemed to have an ownership right in a social media presence built largely through their own efforts. This could not be taken away without the platform showing just cause.

There is a finance rule forthcoming from the Office of the Comptroller of the Currency that relates to banks and credit companies refusing to do business with certain legal businesses like firearms manufacturers.[68] The Left generates a Woke Mob to harass these financial providers until they cave to the pressure and stop processing transactions or serving as their banks.

The rule will state that only legitimate financial concerns may be used to deny service to an otherwise legal entity. This recognizes the commodity nature of these financial services.

Modern businesses literally can't operate without financial institutions so discrimination must be stopped.

The same argument can be logically applied to social media accounts. They are essential to businesses, public figures, and to the rest of us as a vital means to communicate and share information. The electric company can't deny service based on a person's political affiliation nor can the phone company censor conversations they disapprove of. Why should the social media companied be allowed to do the same thing? We can also show them the power of boycotts. They hate us, but they need us. Conservatives who use their platforms create content that drives views which is how they generate revenue. The Left loves to use or threaten to hurt us with boycotts. Let's give them a dose of their own medicine. Their shareholders and investors will notice if half their customers boycott them.

All we want is a level playing field where ideas can compete on their merits. We have asked nicely but to no avail. Wanting and wishing doesn't make things happen. We need to organize and bring the fight to them.

SAVE OUR KIDS FROM THEIR SCHOOLS

The COVID quarantines had the positive effect of showing America's parents the true nature of the kindergarten through 12th grade education system their children are subjected to. The curriculum and harmful nature of teachers' unions and bureaucracy have been on full display.

We must expand charter schools and bring more opportunities for homeschooling that allow parents to create their own groups to educate their kids. We can't give the Left our children's most formative years and let them indoctrinate our kids to hate us and this country.

Who would be crazy enough to send their kids away 8 hours a day for 13 years to be taught things they fundamentally disagree with? Yet, every Conservative parent whose children are in public schools does exactly that. More than any other factor, that is what is causing the cultural divide we find ourselves in today.

More young people believe the Wokeness doctrine these days because it is baked into the curriculum right next to the little that remains of reading, writing and arithmetic. They get social justice as the basis of everything they are taught. This has been growing more pervasive year after year. Our kids were once taught civics and citizenship, how our country works, and what their role is in keeping it running.

Now they are learning how to tear it down because it is riddled with racism and classism and phobias about every identity group the Left can dream up.

This always infested the universities, but it has now filtered down to LGBTQetc. awareness and anti-racism training starting in kindergarten and elementary schools. Multiple generations of teachers have now been through the college training mill and it is these true believers who have the undivided attention of our children while we are at work.

We can counter this ourselves after school and in the evenings, but that's fighting a losing battle. It's a few hours a day versus the eight hours they are in school. We're letting them train our kids as the demolition crew of America. That just paves the way for the creation of a destined-to-fail quasi-socialist bleep hole out of the wreckage of what was formerly known as the United States.

Teachers unions exposed that they only care about power and their budgets when they refused to come back to work, claiming COVID-19 made it too dangerous. These very folks who love to howl about "follow the science" ignored clear science showing that children are not the vector of the virus.

One of the most egregious examples of their hypocrisy was a Chicago teachers' union leader who rallied her troops via a Zoom conference call to resist going back to work because it's not safe while sitting poolside at a Caribbean resort luxuriating.[69] The very idea of public school teachers having unions is a major part of the problem. The best can't be rewarded or the worst fired because the unions hold all the power.

The hypocrisy of the education racket became clear to many parents bearing the brunt of teaching their kids. The system abandoned them and said, "Take care of your own kids, oh but please do keep those sweet tax dollars flowing our way." Parents were forced to pull the weight of these slackers throughout 2020 and into 2021.

We won't win this battle if our children are taught to hate the very freedoms that make America exceptional and even worse that the entire country is based on hate. That is a perversion of history and our progress as a nation. But let's not censor it, let's just stop funding and patronizing it.

Our public education system is a wholly-owned subsidiary of the Left. The teachers' unions and universities have a stranglehold on who gets into the business and what they must believe to teach. We can't overcome that in a frontal assault, so we need to flank it.

Charter schools and home schooling are a start. Anything that gets kids out of the propaganda pipeline helps. The education establishment fights these tooth and nail because they know they can't compete out in the open which threatens their stranglehold on budgets. When shown that better teachers with less administration produce higher quality schooling, the bloated bureaucracy looks bad in comparison.

One of the most effective ideas is more school choice for parents and letting the money follow the kids. If parents are home schooling, they should get a tax break. We do need a baseline to ensure all kids in America are provided a thorough education, but that shouldn't limit those parents who want to go above and beyond for their own children. School choice would also change the education dynamic and make possible better education for kids from lower economic backgrounds. They would be able to get away from a system that has been failing them for 50 years.

We need to be systematic in circumventing the university system. We need a parallel track for people who want to work a trade and earn a good living. It used to be called vocational technical education. That's part of it, but here is where we can steal the game from the Liberals: We need to include information workers on our team.

The Leftist game is requiring the credential of a bachelor's degree in order to be a professional in most career fields. This forces our youth to endure years inside those indoctrination factories to get their social justice vaccinations along with their computer science degrees.

Intersectional gender studies does not improve the quality of code. Just ask any competent software engineer and they will tell you that. There has always been a case for a broadly-based education. The word liberal in the title liberal arts degree wasn't intended to be liberal versus conservative. The Left saw the opportunity and ran with it and they haven't stopped running yet.

Making a split between producers and parasites is important. It can be a newly minted lane for those who will be making real things, providing real services, and making the machinery of our country run. This is not pretending we don't need bureaucrats, administrators, and the myriad of other soft skills. It is a call, however, to stop letting the Left brainwash our productive class with ideas that are incredibly non-productive.

Recognizing there's a problem, it's our responsibility to liberate these soon-to-be productive citizens from the clutches of the Woke Mob. We owe them that much.

CORPORATIONS PAY DANEGELD TO THE MOB

Each one hopes that if he feeds the crocodile enough, the crocodile will eat him last.—Sir Winston Churchill.[70]

Too many major corporations are caught up appeasing the Woke crocodile, hoping it eats them last. They are finding out putting social justice above wise business practices will crash the whole enterprise. The wisdom they are learning is "Get Woke, Go Broke." In an unprecedented and egregious attack on free speech, Twitter banned the accounts of many Conservatives, including the President of the United States, in the days following the incident at the Capitol. By January 14, 2021, Twitter stock dropped 11%. So, about that crocodile….

We need to continue this momentum. We need professionals in most walks of life but they shouldn't be forced to capitulate to the political correctness demanded by the Left. Not even everyone on the Left wants to be dominated by these extreme Liberal values. Fear of the Woke Mob, however, keeps them toeing the politically correct party line. These corporations need to see the damage they are doing to their own productivity by allowing the Left to force them into becoming laboratories for social engineering.

They can escape this by building and funding a for-profit set of academies to provide the professional technical and engineering staff they need. This can also avoid a bonus helping of protests every month when one group micro-aggresses another. We must teach that merit is what gets advancement and that skin color, gender or any other identity politics victim grouping will neither help nor hinder a person.

Even some Woke corporations like Google have already begun offering funding and classes for those who want to learn just the skills needed to do the job.[71] Google realized they are more attuned to the rapidly-changing technical environment than universities. Colleges are weighed down by massive institutional inertia and committees to study the efficiency of their committees. Tech firms can see where the shortfalls are and spin up new programs at the speed of business not bureaucracy.

Most corporations are currently operating with the yoke of Wokeness similarly slowing them down. Programs like Google's help change that dynamic by bringing in workers who focus on competence, not a collection of micro-aggressions and grievances.

We will need to accept that the bulk of the liberal arts–degreed cohort probably won't be interested in being members of our coalition of the productive for now. There are productive people who took advantage of a liberal education in the old-school way by learning to think, study problems, and understand opposing views. Unfortunately, those people are far outnumbered by the people who have been indoctrinated with the anti-capitalist, social justice poison. Sadly, the educated masses who don't fully buy it are scared to oppose it.

They are the technocrat and bureaucrat classes who shepherd the oppressed victim groups. They build the safe spaces where they distribute the takings from the productive class (us). They are not our allies and we should begin to shun them in the same ways they have done to us. It's sad, but we need to move further apart before we can ever come back together.

The Right is now the party where workers of every kind from

farm to factory and even future technologies belong. They are joining us in droves now as the Left makes workplaces just as intolerant and indoctrinated as the rest of their brave, new Liberal world. Let's build an alternative pipeline for those who want to think for themselves and work for the benefit of themselves and their own families.

MAKING OUR OWN CULTURE POPULAR

We must create alternative sources of entertainment. All Hollywood-generated content is infused with social justice Wokeness and anti-conservative messaging. We need to support and patronize the new breed of Conservative creators making shows and movies with positive messages. That means making some of the same kinds of things Hollywood does, but with conservative wisdom embedded. It must appeal to the masses to be effective. We can't just preach to our own choir.

This is not a new idea, but in the current media and entertainment environment it is much more achievable. The advent of streaming services has broken the monopoly that broadcast networks had on TV. More and more people get their news and entertainment from alternative sources. These sources may seem to be run by different people, but, in fact, they are different groupings of the same Liberals.

Don't be discouraged. There are glimmers of hope. One of the first alternative content sources was religious organizations who were justifiably fed up with the depravity that makes up the bulk of popular culture. They began making movies and programs with positive religious values and viewpoints.

Positive and powerful Conservative and spiritual messaging are wonderful things and have drawn more creative people into producing this type of material. It has also brought in people who want to make the types of programming that appeals to a broader audience. This can open the possibility of making religious content relevant, interesting, and in context with the rest of modern culture.

In addition, we must compete in the arena of secular entertainment. Action movies, science fiction, romantic comedies, and every other genre should not be the sole playground for the Hollywood Liberals. They are fundamentally incapable of creating anything without injecting their amoral and anti-conservative views. There are no neutral products coming to market, all of them have at least a few core values of Wokeness presented as the way "good' people think.

We need to play that game, too. We can make action movies where the hero isn't depraved in some way or the characters who represent the Right aren't presented as intolerant, ignorant bigots. We can make standard action flicks that include likeable characters who exemplify Conservative, religious, political, and patriotic American values.

That is one of the main tools of the Left. They began with a few characters who fit their identity politics victim groups. A gay character here, an environmental activist there, and gave them standing as the moral examples of how and who we should all aspire to. The Liberal creatives have amped this up in the current atmosphere of Wokeness. Every production now must have their entire rainbow of human existence both in skin color, gender and sexual proclivity.

Previously there was legitimately a problem with underrepresentation of some groups in popular culture. But now the tables have turned and every show has the banner of Wokeness carried by an unrealistic number of characters representing these no longer marginalized groups.

Saying that is not an indictment of the individuals represented or a call for any kind of discrimination or bigotry. It's simply a recognition that popular culture is the best avenue to effect change in our society. The Left uses it and we should too. We can make products featuring a strong Conservative Black woman or a drama where the Latino family relies on their deep religious beliefs to make it through tough times.

Our coalition on the Right can be every bit as diverse as that of the Left. Let's highlight that.

There is also a huge opportunity to make comedies poking humor at the politically correct Left and their crazy views on climate and micro-aggressions, etc. They are literally self-mocking caricatures of formerly intelligent people these days.

Comedian Ryan Long has been making hilarious videos showing the absurd hypocrisy of the Left. One of his most popular clips has a Woke Lefty sharing common cause with an unrepentant racist over their views. The video depicts two friends, Brad and Chad, one "Woke" and one "racist," agreeing on very fundamental parts of their ideologies:

> Your racial identity is the most important thing. Everything should be looked at through the lens of race, the men say before one of them jinxes another.[72]

He points out how the soft bigotry of low expectations that leads the Left to believe minorities are incapable of doing things like getting a voter ID dovetails nicely with actual racist beliefs about inferiority. It fits right in with a popular online meme showing a Nazi SS officer coming to an unanticipated conclusion as he asks, "Are we the Baddies?"

Actually, yes. Liberals are the baddies. They are a collection of intolerant and oppressive tyrants who want to force everyone to conform to their beliefs. That is wonderful fodder for satire and comedy, so let's get at it. The surest way to weaken an opponent is to get people to laugh at them. That's what they have been doing to us for decades, it's time we return the favor.

We have already made inroads in documentary films. Dinesh D'Souza has been making movies that are reaching larger and larger audiences and has now branched out into popular film. His action thriller, *Infidel,* starring Jim Caviezel, grossed over $4M in the U.S. Kevin Sorbo has also made several successful films including *God's Not Dead* and *Let There be Light* that crossed over from a purely religious audience. Ben Shapiro recently announced his Daily Wire media operation will begin producing TV programs and films that carry conservative messages beginning with action thriller *Run, Hide, Fight* in mid-January 2021.

The Left has caricatured conservatives as knuckle-dragging, bigoted troglodytes for far too long. We need to flip the game, show what we truly represent, and shine a spotlight on the ugliness that taking political correctness too far can really bring.

TAKE CONTROL OF THE POLITICAL RIGHT

The establishment has shown how to fail for far too many years. Some inroads have been made, but it is still largely the domain of risk-averse types who lack the fighting spirit it takes to win a conflict. President Trump showed America will respond to someone who goes out on a limb and stands up for what they believe. Those people need to be more involved in running the Conservative party.

That does not mean excluding the Republican establishment. Part of the challenge is keeping our tent big and then expanding it even bigger. We need to completely refrain from zealot-style tests of how conservative someone is. That mentality is counterproductive and would inevitably splinter us. The Right has been historically bad about demonizing its own for purity infractions. A Conservative who agrees with every party platform but supports a woman's right to choose abortion shouldn't be cast off the island. We must find a way to make common cause with people we share 80+% of core beliefs with because we share near 0% with the Left. We need allies, not purists.

SECOND AMENDMENT GUARANTEES ALL THE REST

We have already heard from the Left that they want to send Beto O'Rourke door to door to collect all our scary guns. The DC v. Heller ruling makes that very difficult, but they will still make a run at it. We must be locked and loaded to respond, figuratively.

I am a huge supporter of the Second Amendment. *Molon labe* "come and take them" is attributed to the vastly outnumbered Spartans in response to the demand by Xerxes I that they surrender their weapons at the Battle of Thermopylae in 480 BC. It's not just a slogan to me, it's a defensive position supported by the Constitution.

The right to keep and bear arms is the place where our last resort against tyranny is stored. God forbid we ever have to use it, but God save anyone in the way if we are ever pushed to that point.

Which we have not yet been by a long shot.

They are trying to shut down gun manufacturers and ammunition producers and the creative forces of the Left will come up with every attack vector they can. We must be vigilant and uncompromising.

FUNDAMENTAL TRANSFORMATION FROM THE RIGHT

The Left loves to claim what we propose is a return is to a White male–dominated world where women, minorities, and the LGBTetc. crowd are oppressed. The TV show *Handmaid's Tale* about a dystopian patriarchy has inspired some of the whackier Liberal activists to protest by wearing red robes and the white nun-like hat of the Handmaids.

Not what we're talking about. The first thing to understand about modern Conservatism is that real tolerance resides on the Right. Wait just a minute for the Liberal heads to stop exploding at that absurd and, yes, evil statement. Wokeness has tolerance for everyone except people who don't passionately agree 100% with them. Those people must be expunged from the face of the earth.

The Right is much more Libertarian these days. It's the "live and let live" and "just leave me alone" mentality. This has come about partly as the reality of actual equality crystallized and as it turned out the world didn't end when a Black dude became President or when gays joined the military.

I publicly supported gays in the military before Barack Obama did. I wrote a public letter signed by a lot of prominent veterans stating that Don't Ask Don't Tell was insulting and stupid. The policy basically said it was OK to be gay in the Army, just don't act gay. Most people shared the opinion at that point of Don't Ask Don't Care. The letter garnered a lot of attention from the Left since most of the signers were well-known Conservatives.

The media picked up my quote:

> If I am lying by the road bleeding, I don't care if the medic coming
> to save me is gay. I just hope he is one of those buff gay guys who

are always in the gym so he can throw me over his shoulder and get me out of there.[73]

Even then, there were many who cautioned that the Left would use that issue to open a passage for transgender troops, as well. Ten years ago, that seemed far-fetched. Now we are right in the middle of a fight over whether the military should pay for active duty personnel to get sex change operations. As it turns out those people who warned me were right.

The issue for gays serving was how other service members would deal with that. While personal feelings can affect the esprit de corps of units, it turned out to be mostly a non-issue. The problem of transgender troops and sex change operations is the extended period of time they are not duty ready and the hormonal drugs causing dangerous emotional and mental issues. It is a combat readiness concern not a social issue. The military mission doesn't matter to the Woke warriors, feelz come first.

We need to be careful about just what changes we make. We can't make everyone feelz good.

There is always pushback when the post-World War II prosperity is mentioned as an ideal time in the U.S. It clearly wasn't ideal for those who were oppressed. The nostalgic reminiscence when people ponder that era is not about a return to oppression. It is about a return to the values and norms that made this country prosperous and, yes, great.

This is updated with the understanding that this must apply to everyone equally and we may even have to pay extra attention to some who were left behind. This does not mean an acquiescence to the Left's plan to game outcomes, pick new winners, use quotas, and even implement reverse racism.

It's just a promise to look around and make sure we are living up to equality of opportunity.

NATIONAL DIVORCE—THE GREAT BREAK UP

Five years ago, I laughed at people who talked about the United States becoming separate countries. I mocked those who said there could be a civil war in our lifetime. I was wrong. Now I talk with serious people about how many countries we would become and where we would locate our Galt's Gulch similar to the utopian community of producers Ayn Rand described.

An actual national divorce is still highly improbable. There are too many logistical, legal, and other issues to deal with like who gets the national debt? I do stake a claim to Barbra Streisand's mansion in Malibu if we do this. I know California belongs to the Left, but we should take some chunks of it for embassies, too. What are they gonna do, fight us for it? That wouldn't go well for them.

We are working on this counterattack to prevent that, but we would be foolish to ignore the possibility. It's good for those on the Left to have to consider what they would do if some day all the places their food comes from left their half of the country.

For the time being we are stuck together. That makes carving back some freedoms from the statist Left a necessity.

RELIGIOUS REVIVAL

America was founded on Judeo-Christian principles and for most of its lifespan this was a positive guiding force for the country and citizens. That has been increasingly less so and the very idea of religious belief, especially Christianity, has been under assault from the Left.

There are some religious people on the Left, but as a political and cultural force there is a strong antipathy toward and even hatred of faith and believers. Liberals worship the secular god of the State and consider it intellectually inferior to believe in the God of the Bible. They have waged war against Christianity using their cultural weapons, but have always run up against that pesky First Amendment in attempts to drive religion from public life.

The principles and moral codes that have always made this country work are strongly based on scripture. We must stand strong and make a case for them as we return this country to glory. There would be no America if brave people hadn't been willing to leave their homelands where they were persecuted and build a better and freer place to live and love God.

Peter speaks of believers this way in the Bible, 1 Peter 1:1:

To God's elect, exiles scattered throughout the provinces of Pontus, Galatia, Cappadocia, Asia and Bithynia.

That isn't a call to build a Christian nation, it means we build a nation where Christians are free to worship and live as God tells us. This same freedom applies to all other religions as well and the coalition of liberty-loving Americans we're building will include people of many faiths. They all shelter under the same Constitutional protection the Left seeks to destroy.

Each person must choose their own way to believe in God, or not. We must also reconcile belief in God with the rules of secular government that runs this country. The Bible also says in Matthew 22:21:

Render therefore unto Caesar the things which are Caesar's; and unto God the things that are God's.

For the purposes of this book, we are dealing mostly on Caesar's side of things. But as in all things God should be guiding your decisions and we must ensure that we never allow Caesar to get onto God's turf either.

The problem the Left has in trying to base their system on purely secular principles is the lack of moral absolutes. They can't bring themselves to declare there is right and wrong and those things come from God. In a multi-cultural society like ours now, that means someone can't just hold the Bible up as the basis for societal morality. But one can, and should, hold it up as a better example than *Das Kapital* by Karl Marx.

There are efforts underway to get the Biden Administration to decertify Christian schools and universities.

The *Blueprint* states, Language regarding accreditation of religious institutions of higher education in the Higher Education Opportunity Act could be interpreted to require accrediting bodies to accredit religious institutions that discriminate or do not meet science-based curricula standards. The Department of Education should issue a regulation clarifying that this provision, which requires accreditation agencies to 'respect the stated mission' of religious institutions, does not require the accreditation of religious institutions that do not meet neutral accreditation standards including nondiscrimination policies and scientific curriculum requirements.[74]

This is a straightforward attempt to use state power to attack religious believers in the practice of their faith. It uses the language of Wokeness to reference non-discrimination policies and "science-based" curricula standards. Those are ways to get at religious objections to trans-gender activism that states a man can become a woman by simply saying so. The science they cite to support that has a bigger argument with the science of biology than with religious belief.

The ideology of Wokeness requires not just acceptance or tolerance, but adherence to their morality and reality-free worldviews. You must profess your acceptance of 57 genders or you will be shamed and shunned. The truly and sadly ironic thing is the enforcers of Wokeness quite deeply resemble the fanatics of the Spanish Inquisition. Confess your sins, repent, and then atone by pushing the radical agenda to your own detriment or you get the rack.

They make the Puritans look tame and they cannot be allowed to dictate that religious beliefs no longer belong in America. The thought police they want to unleash on all of us for ungood thoughts have a special distaste for religious tenets. The nice thing about pushing back on the entire Orwellian system of Wokeness is the return of free exercise of religion right along with speech.

Religious belief and the people who practice it are a powerful force for good on our team. We must always stand up for that. It's a tremendous example of how goodness matters.

STRIVING FOR BETTER OUTCOMES FOR BLACKS IN CITIES UNDER DEMOCRAT RULE

The first thing to do would be end the Democrat rule. That has been the engine of destruction in many of our major metropolises.

We need to strongly make the point that more government handouts will not fix broken cities. That takes the overhaul we have discussed of culture and expectations among the citizens of those cities. We should be reaching out and saying to them, "Do you want more of this? Because we have a better way and you are invited."

All the most crime-laden, economically failing major cities are run by Democrats and have been for decades. They have had every opportunity to prove their ideas work and yet the poor suffer and crime festers. Decent people everywhere recoil when they see all this. The riots and looting have been a crystal-clear view into the culture created when told nothing is your fault, it's all the result of this invisible nemesis that keeps you down. The Left say that is Systemic Racism but we can fairly point out that living under Democrat rule is the actual culprit.

When the 2020 riots began, the Democrat-ruled cities where they were happening gave their law enforcement agencies orders to stand down. They let the mobs run rampant hoping to dampen the tensions. How'd that work out? Bullies see tolerance as weakness. As soon as they felt no resistance, the rioters pulled out all the stops and haven't stopped yet.

Once they burned their own neighborhoods they moved uptown and looted the designer shops, you know, for racial justice. Watching the mob pillage and plunder the Chanel and Louis Vuitton stores on Chicago's Magnificent Mile in the name of racial justice was mindboggling. The mob is not about to let the pressure up. There were plenty more Chanel bags to loot. Why stop?

The side of law and order is literally battling state and local government as well as the looters and rioters. It makes it legitimate to wonder if the major cities are just a lost cause. It's hard to say no, because it's difficult to see how it is going to get any better.

Black people prosper where they follow the time-tested rules of staying in school, not having kids too young, and two-parent care of children. That is one of the main paths out of poverty to prosperity and it doesn't care about the color of skin. Living under Democrat rule creates a culture in these communities that devalues school and rewards having children out of wedlock. It creates a permanent client victim class and that won't change just because they invented the boogeyman of Systemic Racism.

The hard part is selling a message that says stay in school, work hard, and put off personal gratification until later. Several generations have now been trained by the Left to distrust the system and to believe that a person is not responsible if they fail. Add it to a culture that considers staying in school acting White and selling out, and hero-worships men who have babies with multiple women yet fail to take care of them. That's a huge systemic problem for sure but it isn't racism.

The Democrats don't actually want this fixed because they need the self-downtrodden as perpetual marketing tools. They point to them as proof the system is racist and demand more state power to fix the game that they claim is rigged against them. Anti-theist Christopher Hitchens served as the Devil's Advocate (a real thing not a pun) at the canonization hearings for Mother Teresa as her potential sainthood was debated. He pointed out that she kept several of her facilities in wretched condition and the patients there largely untreated so she could use them to show donors.

Democrat-run cities serve the same purpose. Decades of rule by a party that combines bad policies with incompetence and corruption ensures that the downtrodden will always be there to show donors, voters, and politicians. The trick they get away with is blaming Systemic Racism rather than their own malfeasance and policies that discourage personal responsibility.

The Right has a huge advantage in the battle for hearts and minds of the country: Most of the policies that Wokeness recommends have been tried and failed in major Democrat-governed cities. The schools are sub-standard, the city-wide crime rates are through the roof, and the quality of life is so low it's surprising people choose to remain there.

Chicago, Philadelphia, Detroit, St. Louis, and Baltimore are all horrible places to live unless a person is an upper middle class professional who can hide in the pockets of prosperity amid the filth. They have been run into the ground by the policies Wokeness wants to double down on.

Democrats have been in power in:

Chicago since 1927

Philadelphia since 1952

St. Louis since 1961

Detroit since 1962

Baltimore since 1967

The Woke activists would say this is not representative of their new and improved Leftist agenda. Their program is to blow right past Liberalism and head to the sweet embrace of Socialism. The problem is that's the only governing ideology with a worse track record than Liberal Democrats. It has an unblemished record of death, destruction, and despair leading to economic collapse and starving people.

There is not a single example of successful Socialism anywhere in the world or any time in history. They try to claim the previous successes of the Scandinavian countries who managed to run Social Democracies for a large part of the post-World War II era. Those, however, were small countries with a homogeneous population that largely shared an agreement to work together and have a strong social services backbone. They are now struggling to maintain that with declining birth rates and an influx of refugees with high unemployment rates straining the resources of the system.[75]

There's no doubt a Black kid born in Baltimore, Chicago, or Detroit starts off in a big hole to climb out of. There is currently not enough incentive to climb out and like crabs in a bucket, their own peers will try to drag them back in if they seem to be getting out. There is no simple solution that will turn this around. Before any of the principles that help people of any color out of poverty will work, the mindset and culture have to change. We must stop the Left from enabling the cycle of self-destruction with policies that lack accountability. We must end the message that says it's not your fault, it's the racist system.

Black people have been running those "racist systems" in those cities for decades. We can certainly make that point and offer a hand to help their poorly-served constituents.

CONCLUSION

WE ARE IN A BAD PLACE as a nation and especially for those of us on the political Right. But we can change that if we focus, build and present a positive alternative to the failures and oppression of the Left.

That is the plan we have shown in this book. Now we need to take that message to our families, friends and neighbors. A revival for America is underway and we're bringing it.

We are decades, even generations, behind in the American Cold War that the Left has been waging to fundamentally transform the country. After World War II, we took on the massive challenge of defeating the Soviet Union and they took on the massive challenge of turning America into a Socialist paradise.

We won our fight and the Soviets' attempt at Global Communism is on the ash heap of history. The Left is winning their fight, except there is no such thing as a Socialist paradise. But they gained control of our education system, popular culture, and government bureaucracy.

They have taken us to the brink of state control and a long slide into an economic death spiral.

If we plan to continue living together as citizens of the same country, we need to either claw back some control of these or build our own parallel systems. If not, they will push us to the margins of society. So, let's do that. We built all of the good things in this country before they coopted them. We can do it again.

They have relied on our natural tendencies as law-abiding citizens to take their assaults on our freedoms and smears against us without retaliating. The Storming of the Capitol may signal the end of that period unless we can get things moving the right direction. A person doesn't have to agree with any of the claims about the election being stolen to understand that was far from the only reason for the protest.

The entire assault of Wokeness on our great country is an affront to freedom-loving people. The use of it to demonize our beliefs and way of life is intolerable. Damn right we're mad and that will continue to boil over until enough of these issues are addressed.

The months-long rampage where BLM and Antifa did billions of dollars in damage to make a political point was just fine with the Left. It was righteous anger from a protected victim class. It was Wokeness in action. When a crowd of Conservative protestors went too far and busted into the U.S. Capitol, you'd think the world was ending. The howls of indignation and the crying about an attempted coup were way out of proportion to the actual offense.

We have an arduous road ahead. We either create a new and better Conservative party now or lose to the Left's Woke agenda. They pose a mortal threat to the future of the United States. We need to put hope back in the heart of the Right and unify as a party before that escalates into an active Second Civil War.

But we can do that. We're not about to lose to a bunch of over-educated, under-capable clowns who wouldn't survive 15 minutes outside their bubble. We are the muscles and spine of this country and also the part of its brain not addled by foolishness. That and our patriotic and freedom-loving spirit gives us the advantage we need to push on to victory.

We are the greatest country this planet has ever seen. We are the Right, and we are right. And. We. Will. Prevail!

ENDNOTES

1   Thomas, K., & Siddiqui, S. (2021, January 08). Biden Says Rioters Who Stormed Capitol Were Domestic Terrorists. Retrieved January 10, 2021, from https://www.wsj.com/articles/biden-says-mob-that-stormed-capitol-were-domestic-terrorists-11610046962

2   Bowden, E. (2020, June 08). More than 700 officers injured in George Floyd protests across US. Retrieved January 10, 2021, from https://nypost.com/2020/06/08/more-than-700-officers-injured-in-george-floyd-protests-across-us/

3   Bowden, E. (2020, June 08). More than 700 officers injured in George Floyd protests across US. Retrieved January 10, 2021, from https://nypost.com/2020/06/08/more-than-700-officers-injured-in-george-floyd-protests-across-us/

4   Jacobo, J. (2021, January 7). What Trump told supporters. Retrieved January 10, 2021, from https://abcnews.go.com/Politics/trump-told-supporters-stormed-capitol-hill/story?id=75110558

5   Permanent suspension of @realDonaldTrump. (n.d.). Retrieved January 10, 2021, from https://blog.twitter.com/en_us/topics/company/2020/suspension.html

6   Permanent suspension of @realDonaldTrump. (n.d.). Retrieved January 10, 2021, from https://blog.twitter.com/en_us/topics/company/2020/suspension.html

7   Congresswoman Nancy Pelosi. (2003, February 5). Retrieved January 10, 2021, from https://pelosi.house.gov/sites/pelosi.house.gov/files/pressarchives/releases/prPowellStatement020503.html

8   Transcript: Obama's Speech Against The Iraq War. (2009, January 20). Retrieved January 10, 2021, from https://www.npr.org/templates/story/story.php?storyId=99591469

9   Reich, R. (2020, October 17). Robert Reich Truth & reconciliation Tweet. Retrieved January 10, 2021, from https://twitter.com/RBReich/status/1317614803704115200?s=20

10   Hayes, C. (2020, October 06). Chris Hayes Truth and Reconciliation Tweet. Retrieved January 10, 2021, from https://twitter.com/chrislhayes/status/1313291524629770242?s=20

11   CASERTA, M. (2018, March 03). Voters must remember US decline in Obama era. Retrieved January 10, 2021, from https://apnews.com/article/c7c4ee4c39394b5cbbad6a432d86dcc1

12   Preston, M. (2010, January 09). Reid apologizes for racial remarks about Obama during campaign. Retrieved January 10, 2021, from https://www.cnn.com/2010/POLITICS/01/09/obama.reid/index.html

13   Press, A. (2015, March 25). Sen. Joe Biden Expresses Regret Over Barack Obama Comments. Retrieved January 10, 2021, from https://www.foxnews.com/story/sen-joe-biden-expresses-regret-over-barack-obama-comments

14   Fox News. (2015, January 27). Obama calls Florida shooting death 'tragedy,' says his son would 'look like Trayvon'. Retrieved January 10, 2021, from https://www.foxnews.com/politics/obama-calls-florida-shooting-death-tragedy-says-his-son-would-look-like-trayvon

15   CNN. (2016, October 5). CNN ORC Intl Poll on Race. Retrieved January 10, 2021, from http://i2.cdn.turner.com/cnn/2016/images/10/05/race,.justice.pdf.pdf

16   Lee, M. (2018, August 15). 'Hands up, don't shoot' did not happen in Ferguson. Retrieved January 10, 2021, from https://www.washingtonpost.com/news/fact-checker/wp/2015/03/19/hands-up-dont-shoot-did-not-happen-in-ferguson/

17   McFarland, K. (2015, July 15). Mr. President, Is America Exceptional? Retrieved January 10, 2021, from https://www.foxnews.com/opinion/mr-president-is-america-exceptional-you-betcha

18   Lowry, R. (2017, December 19). Trump's first year is starting to look like a big win. Retrieved January 10, 2021, from https://nypost.com/2017/12/18/trumps-first-year-is-starting-to-look-like-a-big-win/

19   Staff, P. (2017, August 15). Full text: Trump's comments on white supremacists, 'alt-left' in Charlottesville. Retrieved January 10, 2021, from https://www.politico.com/story/2017/08/15/full-text-trump-comments-white-supremacists-alt-left-transcript-241662

20   Staff, S. (2020, December 04). Ensuring a Valid Election. Retrieved January 10, 2021, from https://securitystudies.org/ensuring-a-valid-election/

21   Staff, I. (2020). Institute for Fair Elections 2020 Prospectus. Retrieved January 10, 2021, from http://instituteforfairelections.org/county-voter-integrity-summary-los-angeles-2/

22   Davidson, J. (2020, October 15). Twitter Censors Again: Blocks Second New York Post Story On Hunter Biden Seeking Cash From Chinese Firm. Retrieved January 10, 2021, from https://thefederalist.com/2020/10/15/twitter-censors-again-blocks-second-new-york-post-story-on-hunter-biden-seeking-cash-from-chinese-firm/

23   Randazzo, S. (2020, November 14). Trump Lawyers Pressured to End Role in Election Challenges. Retrieved January 10, 2021, from https://www.wsj.com/articles/trump-lawyers-pressured-to-end-role-in-election-challenges-11605371893

24   Staff, S. (2021, January 02). Joint Statement from Senators Cruz, Johnson, Lankford, Daines, Kennedy, Blackburn, Braun, Senators-Elect Lummis, Marshall, Hagerty, Tuberville. Retrieved January 10, 2021, from https://www.cruz.senate.gov/?p=press_release&id=5541

25   Haberman, M. (2021, January 07). Trump Told Crowd 'You Will Never Take Back Our Country With Weakness'. Retrieved January 10, 2021, from https://www.nytimes.com/2021/01/06/us/politics/trump-speech-capitol.html

26   Coleman, J. (2021, January 07). Liz Cheney blames Trump for riots: 'He lit the flame'. Retrieved January 10, 2021, from https://thehill.com/homenews/house/533024-liz-cheney-blames-trump-for-riots-he-lit-the-flame

27 Cohen, Z. (2021, January 07). CNN officially characterizing today's violence on Capitol Hill today as domestic terrorism. Retrieved January 10, 2021, from https://twitter.com/ZcohenCNN/status/1346995206269194240?s=20

28 Wulfsohn, J. (2020, August 27). CNN panned for on-air graphic reading 'fiery but mostly peaceful protest' in front of Kenosha fire. Retrieved January 10, 2021, from https://www.foxnews.com/media/cnn-panned-for-on-air-graphic-reading-fiery-but-mostly-peaceful-protest-in-front-of-kenosha-fire

29 Wulfsohn, J. (2020, May 29). MSNBC's Ali Velshi says situation not 'generally speaking unruly' while standing outside burning building. Retrieved January 10, 2021, from https://www.foxnews.com/media/msnbc-anchor-says-minneapolis-carnage-is-mostly-a-protest-as-building-burns-behind-him

30 Fiene, H. (2015, April 06). Gay Marriage Isn't About Justice, It's About Selma Envy. Retrieved January 10, 2021, from https://thefederalist.com/2015/03/31/gay-marriage-isnt-about-justice-its-about-selma-envy/

31 Wulfsohn, J. (2020, September 21). Black Lives Matter removes 'What We Believe' website page calling to 'disrupt ... nuclear family structure'. Retrieved January 10, 2021, from https://www.foxnews.com/media/black-lives-matter-disrupt-nuclear-family-website

32 Richardson, V. (2020, June 04). Eye-gouging and PowerPoint: Project Veritas infiltrates Antifa in undercover video. Retrieved January 10, 2021, from https://www.washingtontimes.com/news/2020/jun/4/eye-gouging-and-powerpoint-project-veritas-infiltr/

33 Army, U. (2020). Primary Special Forces Missions. Retrieved January 10, 2021, from http://goarmy.com/special-forces/primary-missions.html

34 Framers, T. (1787). U.S. Constitution - Second Amendment: Resources: Constitution Annotated: Congress.gov: Library of Congress. Retrieved January 10, 2021, from https://constitution.congress.gov/constitution/amendment-2/

35 Scalia, A. (2007, October). DC v. Heller opinion. Retrieved January 10, 2021, from https://www.supremecourt.gov/opinions/07pdf/07-290.pdf

36 McReynolds, J. (1939). United States v. Miller Opinion. Retrieved January 10, 2021, from https://www.oyez.org/cases/1900-1940/307us174

37 Scalia, A. (2007, October). DC v. Heller opinion. Retrieved January 10, 2021, from https://www.supremecourt.gov/opinions/07pdf/07-290.pdf

38 BATF, U. (1934). National Firearms Act- Bureau of Alcohol, Tobacco, Firearms and Explosives. Retrieved January 10, 2021, from https://www.atf.gov/rules-and-regulations/national-firearms-act

39 Koper, C. (2004). Updated Assessment of the Federal Assault Weapons Ban: Impacts on Gun Markets and Gun Violence, 1994-2003. Retrieved January 10, 2021, from https://www.ncjrs.gov/App/Publications/abstract.aspx?ID=204431

40 Scalia, A. (2007, October). DC v. Heller opinion. Retrieved January 10, 2021, from https://www.supremecourt.gov/opinions/07pdf/07-290.pdf

41 Scalia, A. (2007, October). DC v. Heller opinion. Retrieved January 10, 2021, from https://www.supremecourt.gov/opinions/07pdf/07-290.pdf

42 Scalia, A. (2007, October). DC v. Heller opinion. Retrieved January 10, 2021, from https://www.supremecourt.gov/opinions/07pdf/07-290.pdf

43 Congress, U. (1956). 10 U.S. Code § 246 - Militia: Composition and classes. Retrieved January 10, 2021, from https://www.law.cornell.edu/uscode/text/10/246

44 Staff, S. (2020, July 07). The Epidemic of Police Killings that wasn't. Retrieved January 10, 2021, from https://securitystudies.org/the-epidemic-of-police-killings-that-wasnt/

45   Hay, A. (2020, August 15). Right-wing groups clash with counter protesters in several U.S. states. Retrieved January 10, 2021, from https://www.reuters.com/article/us-global-race-protests-stone-mountain/right-wing-groups-clash-with-counter-protesters-in-several-u-s-states-idUSKCN25B115

46   Phillips, M. (2021, January 07). Capitol Police officer 'didn't have a choice' in shooting Babbitt, GOP congressman says. Retrieved January 10, 2021, from https://www.foxnews.com/politics/capitol-police-officer-shooting-ashli-babbitt-gop-congressman

47   Cod, U. (1999). 1999 US Code :: Title 18 - CRIMES AND CRIMINAL PROCEDURE :: PART I - CRIMES :: CHAPTER 115 - TREASON, SEDITION, AND SUBVERSIVE ACTIVITIES :: Sec. 2383 - Rebellion or insurrection. Retrieved January 13, 2021, from https://law.justia.com/codes/us/1999/title18/parti/chap115/sec2383

48   Code, U. (1999). 1999 US Code :: Title 18 - CRIMES AND CRIMINAL PROCEDURE :: PART I - CRIMES :: CHAPTER 115 - TREASON, SEDITION, AND SUBVERSIVE ACTIVITIES :: Sec. 2384 - Seditious conspiracy. Retrieved January 13, 2021, from https://law.justia.com/codes/us/1999/title18/parti/chap115/sec2384/

49   Congress, U. (2018). 18 U.S. Code § 2331 - Definitions. Retrieved January 10, 2021, from https://www.law.cornell.edu/uscode/text/18/2331

50   Staff, J. (2021). Message from Joint Chiefs of Staff. Retrieved January 13, 2021, from https://www.navy.mil/Resources/NAVADMINs/Message/Article/2469695/message-to-the-joint-force/

51   Constitution, U. (1787). Sixth Amendment. Retrieved January 10, 2021, from https://www.law.cornell.edu/constitution/sixth_amendment

52   Stanford Law Review. (2020, December 04). 'Forseeable Violence' & Black Lives Matter. Retrieved January 10, 2021, from https://www.stanfordlawreview.org/online/forseeable-violence-black-lives-matter/

53   Sebelius, S. (2017, February 23). Leaders need to encourage calm, not pander, in BLM controversy. Retrieved January 10, 2021, from https://www.reviewjournal.com/uncategorized/leaders-need-to-encourage-calm-not-pander-in-blm-controversy/

54   DOJ. (2020, September 21). Department Of Justice Identifies New York City, Portland And Seattle As Jurisdictions Permitting Violence And Destruction Of Property. Retrieved January 10, 2021, from https://www.justice.gov/opa/pr/department-justice-identifies-new-york-city-portland-and-seattle-jurisdictions-permitting

55   Kruse, B. (2020, June 30). CHOP: Seattle mayor walks back 'summer of love' comment. Retrieved January 10, 2021, from https://www.q13fox.com/news/chop-seattle-mayor-walks-back-summer-of-love-comment

56   Patty, B. (2020, October 07). A Theory of the Militia. Retrieved January 10, 2021, from https://securitystudies.org/a-theory-of-the-militia/

57   DoD, U. (2018). Joint Publication 3-24 Counterinsurgency. Retrieved January 10, 2021, from Joint Publication 3-24 Counterinsurgency

58   Seattle, B. (2020, September 23). Our Demands- Black Lives Matter. Retrieved January 10, 2021, from https://blacklivesseattle.org/our-demands/

59   DEFUND THE POLICE. (n.d.). Retrieved January 10, 2021, from https://m4bl.org/defund-the-police/

60   Marx, K. (2020, December 12). From each according to his ability, to each according to his needs. Retrieved January 10, 2021, from https://en.wikipedia.org/wiki/From_each_according_to_his_ability,_to_each_according_to_his_needs

61   Jr., M. (2019, January 25). "I Have a Dream," Address Delivered at the March on Washington for Jobs and Freedom. Retrieved January 10, 2021, from https://kinginstitute.stanford.edu/king-papers/documents/i-have-dream-address-delivered-march-washington-jobs-and-freedom

62   Kast, M. (2020, June 04). Cheerleader who used racial slur on social media will not attend University of Tennessee. Retrieved January 10, 2021, from https://www.knoxnews.com/story/news/education/2020/06/04/cheerleader-who-used-racial-slur-will-not-attend-university-of-tennessee/3147231001/

63   Staff, I. (2020, June 24). Jimmy Kimmel and Jimmy Fallon Apologize for Blackface Sketches. Retrieved January 10, 2021, from https://www.insideedition.com/media/videos/jimmy-kimmel-and-jimmy-fallon-apologize-for-blackface-sketches-60327

64   Buckley, W. F., Jr. (2019, September 03). Our Mission Statement. Retrieved January 14, 2021, from https://www.nationalreview.com/1955/11/our-mission-statement-william-f-buckley-jr/

65   Trump, D. (2020). Executive Order on Combating Race and Sex Stereotyping. Retrieved January 10, 2021, from https://www.whitehouse.gov/presidential-actions/executive-order-combating-race-sex-stereotyping/

66   Ekins, E. (2020, October 20). Poll: 62% of Americans Say They Have Political Views They're Afraid to Share. Retrieved January 11, 2021, from https://www.cato.org/publications/survey-reports/poll-62-americans-say-they-have-political-views-theyre-afraid-share

67   Staff, F. (2020). Antitrust lawsuit against Facebook. Retrieved January 10, 2021, from https://www.ftc.gov/system/files/documents/cases/1910134fbcomplaint.pdf

68   OCC, S. (2020, November 20). Proposed Rule Would Ensure Fair Access to Bank Services, Capital, and Credit. Retrieved January 10, 2021, from https://www.occ.gov/news-issuances/news-releases/2020/nr-occ-2020-156.html

69   Bradley, B. (2021, January 01). CTU board member facing criticism for vacationing in Caribbean while pushing remote learning. Retrieved January 10, 2021, from https://wgntv.com/news/wgn-investigates/ctu-board-member-facing-criticism-for-vacationing-in-caribbean-while-pushing-remote-learning/

70   Churchill, W. (1940, January 20). The War Situation: House Of Many Mansions. Retrieved January 15, 2021, from https://winstonchurchill.org/resources/speeches/1940-the-finest-hour/the-war-situation-house-of-many-mansions/

71   Staff, G. (2020). Professional Certificate Training Programs. Retrieved January 10, 2021, from https://grow.google/certificates/

72   Davidson, J. (2020, July 20). Hilarious Viral Video Calls Out Hypocrisy In 'Woke' Movement. Retrieved January 10, 2021, from https://thefederalist.com/2020/07/20/hilarious-viral-video-calls-out-hypocrisy-in-woke-movement/

73   Keller, J. (2010, June 18). Military Bloggers and Don't Ask, Don't Tell. Retrieved January 10, 2021, from https://www.theatlantic.com/politics/archive/2010/06/military-bloggers-and-dont-ask-dont-tell/57700/

74   Dreher, R. (2020, November 19). LGBT Lobby Coming After Christian Schools. Retrieved January 10, 2021, from https://www.theamericanconservative.com/dreher/lgbt-lobby-coming-after-christian-schools/

75   Goodman, P. (2019, July 11). The Nordic Model May Be the Best Cushion Against Capitalism. Can It Survive Immigration? Retrieved January 10, 2021, from https://www.nytimes.com/2019/07/11/business/sweden-economy-immigration.html

ACKNOWLEDGMENTS

I want to thank my parents Russ and Jean Hanson for teaching me what is good about America and what I owe for the privilege of living here. Also my daughter Hannah Hanson for her example and inspiring me to want to make the world a better place for the future. And no one deserves more credit than my wonderful wife Samantha Nerove who collaborated with me on all the ideas and contributed many of her own. She also had the thankless task of editing my piles of words into readable fashion.